GOD'S RENEWED CREATION

call to hope and action

- The Pastoral Letter

- The Pastoral Letter for Liturgical Settings

- The Foundation Document

- Guide for Group Study

- Guide for Teachers of Children

COKESBURY / Nashville

Contents

Introduction

Dear Members of The United Methodist Church:

Greetings to you in the name of the Triune God.

The Council of Bishops of The United Methodist Church commends to you these resources for studying the Pastoral Letter and Foundation Document for *God's Renewed Creation: Call to Hope and Action*. We believe that these resources will enable you to have thoughtful discussions with one another which, by the guidance of the Holy Spirit, may result in changes in your lives, our Church, and the world.

One of our primary responsibilities as bishops is to interpret the apostolic faith as it is expressed in Scripture and tradition both evangelically and prophetically (*Book of Discipline*, ¶ 414.3). As requested by the General Conference, and on behalf of the whole Church, we have issued our Pastoral Letter and Foundation Document in order to encourage all of us to respond, according to the perspective of our faith in the living God, to the realities threatening our world. We ask that you receive these statements as our service to the Church and use them to explore these issues and shape your practice as disciples of Jesus Christ our Lord.

We are mindful that Christians in other churches around the world are also making statements about our responsibility before our Creator to care for the creation. It is our prayer that our Christian conversation and action will be taken up and used by the Spirit of God as a part of God's plan for the renewal of all creation.

Sincerely,

Gregory V. Palmer

Bishop Gregory V. Palmer
President, Council of Bishops

Timothy W. Whitaker

Bishop Timothy W. Whitaker
Convener, Task Force on *God's Renewed Creation: Call to Hope and Action*

God's Renewed Creation: Call to Hope and Action

The Pastoral Letter*

God's creation is in crisis. We, the Bishops of The United Methodist Church, cannot remain silent while God's people and God's planet suffer. This beautiful natural world is a loving gift from God, the Creator of all things seen and unseen. God has entrusted its care to all of us, but we have turned our backs on God and on our responsibilities. Our neglect, selfishness, and pride have fostered:

- pandemic poverty and disease,
- environmental degradation, and
- the proliferation of weapons and violence.[1]

Despite these interconnected threats to life and hope, God's creative work continues. Despite the ways we all contribute to these problems, God still invites each one of us to participate in the work of renewal. We must begin the work of renewing creation by being renewed in our own hearts and minds. *We cannot help the world until we change our way of being in it.*

We all feel saddened by the state of the world, overwhelmed by the scope of these problems, and anxious about the future, but *God calls us and equips us to respond.* No matter how bad things are, God's creative work continues. Christ's resurrection assures us that death and destruction do not have the last word. Paul taught that through Jesus Christ, God offers redemption to all of creation and reconciles all things, "whether on earth or in heaven" (Colossians 1:20[2]). God's Spirit is always and everywhere at work in the world fighting poverty, restoring health, renewing creation, and reconciling peoples.

Aware of God's vision for creation, we no longer see a list of isolated problems affecting disconnected people, plants, and animals. Rather, we see one interconnected system that is "groaning in travail" (Romans 8:22 RSV). The threats to peace, people, and planet earth are related to one another, and God's vision encompasses complete well-being. We, your bishops, join with many global religious leaders to call for a comprehensive response to these interrelated issues. We urge all United Methodists and people of goodwill to offer themselves as instruments of God's renewing Spirit in the world.

---

*The 2004 General Conference of The United Methodist Church called for the Council of Bishops to publish new documents and a study guide similar to the Council's landmark call in 1986, *In Defense of Creation: The Nuclear Crisis and a Just Peace.* This is the Council's response to the General Conference action (*The Book of Resolutions of The United Methodist Church 2004:* "Replace *In Defense of Creation* with new Document and Study Guide").

First, let us orient our lives toward God's holy vision. This vision of the future calls us to hope and to action. "For surely I know the plans I have for you, says the LORD, plans for your welfare and not for harm, to give you a future with hope" (Jeremiah 29:11). Christ's resurrection assures us that this vision is indeed a *promise* of renewal and reconciliation. As disciples of Christ, we take God's promise as the purpose for our lives. Let us, then, rededicate ourselves to God's holy vision, living each day with awareness of the future that God extends to us and of the Spirit that leads us onward.

Second, let us practice social and environmental holiness. We believe personal holiness and social holiness must never be separated. John Wesley preached: "The gospel of Christ knows of no religion, but social. No holiness but social holiness."[3] Through social holiness we make ourselves channels of God's blessing in the world. Because God's blessing, care, and promise of renewal extend to all of creation, we can speak today of "environmental holiness" as well. We practice social and environmental holiness by caring for God's people and God's planet and by challenging those whose policies and practices neglect the poor, exploit the weak, hasten global warming, and produce more weapons.

Third, let us live and act in hope. As people in the tradition of John Wesley, we understand reconciliation and renewal to be part of the *process* of salvation that is already under way. We are not hemmed in to a fallen world. Rather, we are part of a divine unfolding process to which we must contribute. As we faithfully respond to God's grace and call to action, the Holy Spirit guides us in this renewal. With a resurrection spirit, we look forward to the renewal of the whole creation and commit ourselves to that vision. We pray that God will accept and use our lives and resources that we rededicate to a ministry of peace, justice, and hope to overcome poverty and disease, environmental degradation, and the proliferation of weapons and violence.

With God's help and with you as our witnesses—

1. *We as your bishops pledge to answer God's call to deepen our spiritual consciousness as just stewards of creation.* We commit ourselves to faithful and effective leadership on these issues in our denomination and in our communities and nations.

2. *We pledge to make God's vision of renewal our goal.* With every evaluation and decision, we will ask: Does this contribute to God's renewal of creation? Ever aware of the difference between what is and what must be, we pledge to practice Wesleyan "holy dissatisfaction."[4]

3. *We pledge to practice dialogue with those whose life experience differs dramatically from our own, and we pledge to practice prayerful self-examination.* For example, in the Council of Bishops, the fifty active bishops in the United States are committed to listening and learning with the nineteen active bishops in Africa, Asia, and Europe. And the bishops representing the conferences in the United States will prayerfully examine the fact that their nation consumes more than its fair share of the world's resources, generates the most waste, and produces the most weapons.

4. *We pledge ourselves to make common cause with religious leaders and people of goodwill worldwide who share these concerns.* We will connect and collaborate with ecumenical and interreligious partners and with community and faith organizations so that we may strengthen our common efforts.

5. *We pledge to advocate for justice and peace in the halls of power in our respective nations and international organizations.*

6. *We pledge to measure the "carbon footprint"[5] of our episcopal and denominational offices, determine how to reduce it, and implement those changes.* We will urge our congregations, schools, and settings of ministry to do the same.

7. *We pledge to provide, to the best of our ability, the resources needed by our conferences to reduce dramatically our collective exploitation of the planet, peoples, and communities, including technical assistance with buildings and programs, education and training, and young people's and online networking resources.*

8. *We pledge to practice hope as we engage and continue supporting the many transforming ministries of our denomination.* Every day we will thank God for fruit produced through the work of The United Methodist Church and through each of you.

9. *We pledge more effective use of the church and community Web pages to inspire and to share what we learn.* [6] We celebrate the communications efforts that tell the stories of struggle and transformation within our denomination.

With these pledges, we respond to God's gracious invitation to join in the process of renewal. God is already visibly at work in people and groups around the world. We rededicate ourselves to join these movements, the movements of the Spirit. Young people are passionately raising funds to provide mosquito nets for their "siblings" thousands of miles away. Dockworkers are refusing to off-load small weapons being smuggled to armed combatants in civil wars in their continents. People of faith are demanding land reform on behalf of landless farm workers. Children and young people have formed church-wide "green teams" to transform our buildings and ministries into testimonies of stewardship and sustainability. Ecumenical and interreligious partners persist in demanding that the major nuclear powers reduce their arsenals, step by verifiable step, making a way to a more secure world totally disarmed of nuclear weapons. God is already doing a new thing. With this Letter and the accompanying Foundation Document, we rededicate ourselves to participate in God's work, and we urge you all to rededicate yourselves as well.

We beseech every United Methodist, every congregation, and every public leader: *Will you participate in God's renewing work?* We are filled with hope for what God can accomplish through us, and we pray you respond: "We will, with God's help!"

May God's grace purify our reason, strengthen our will, and guide our action. May the love of God, the peace of Christ, and the power of the Holy Spirit be among you, everywhere and always, so that you may be a blessing to all creation and to all the children of God, making peace, nurturing and practicing hope, choosing life, and coming to life eternal. Amen.

Notes

1. In 2002, the Reverend Dr. William Sloane Coffin, referring to a trio of political threats, said, "A more likely and far more dangerous trio would be environmental degradation, pandemic poverty, and a world awash with weapons" (*The Chautauqua Appeal*, with Joan Brown Campbell and Stephen J. Sidorak, Jr.).
2. Scriptural references unless otherwise noted are from the New Revised Standard Version of the Bible copyright 1989, Division of Christian Education of the National Council of the Churches of Christ in the United States of America. Used by permission. All rights reserved.
3. *Hymns and Sacred Poems*, 1739, ¶5.
4. "When . . . Christian perfection becomes the goal, a fundamental hope is aroused that the future can surpass the present. And a corresponding holy dissatisfaction is aroused with regard to any present state of affairs—a dissatisfaction that supplies the critical edge necessary to keep the process of individual transformation moving. Moreover, this holy dissatisfaction is readily transferable from the realm of the individual to that of society, where it provides a persistent motivation for reform in the light of 'a more perfect way' that goes beyond any status quo" (Theodore Runyon, *The New Creation: John Wesley's Theology Today* [Nashville: Abingdon Press, 1998], p. 168).
5. A "carbon footprint" is an estimate of how much carbon dioxide (a greenhouse gas) is produced to support life activities, including travel and home energy use. Carbon footprints are also applied on a larger scale to companies, businesses, and nations.
6. In support of the many persons who have followed this project of the Council, an interactive multimedia Web site will have resources, educational materials, downloadable video clips and social networking: www.hopeandaction.org.

God's Renewed Creation: Call to Hope and Action

The Pastoral Letter for Liturgical Settings*

God's creation is in crisis. We, the bishops of The United Methodist Church, cannot remain silent while God's people and God's planet suffer. This beautiful natural world is a loving gift from God, the Creator of all things seen and unseen. God has entrusted its care to all of us, but we have turned our backs on God and on our responsibilities. Our neglect, selfishness, and pride have fostered:

- pandemic poverty and disease,
- environmental degradation, and
- the proliferation of weapons and violence.[1]

Despite these interconnected threats to life and hope, God's creative work continues. Despite the ways we all contribute to these problems, God still invites each one of us to participate in the work of renewal. We must begin the work of renewing creation by being renewed in our own hearts and minds. *We cannot help the world until we change our way of being in it.*

In preparation for this Letter and the accompanying Foundation Document, we, the bishops, have listened to thousands of United Methodists around the world. You asked us to lead with concrete actions; raise awareness; and offer a word of hope to ease our grief, guilt, and concern. Because you informed the substance of this Letter, we invite you to participate in its reading by joining in the lament, confession, and pledges herein. The differences among us are great, but we share a common concern and a common call. We all feel saddened by the state of the world, overwhelmed by the scope of these problems, and anxious about the future, but *God calls us and equips us to respond.* No matter how bad things are, God's creative work continues.

Christ's resurrection assures us that death and destruction do not have the last word. Paul taught that through Jesus Christ, God offers redemption to all of creation and reconciles all things, "whether on earth or in heaven" (Colossians 1:20[2]). God's Spirit is always and everywhere at work in the world fighting poverty, restoring health, renewing creation, and reconciling peoples.

---

*The 2004 General Conference of The United Methodist Church called for the Council of Bishops to publish new documents and a study guide similar to the Council's landmark call in 1986, *In Defense of Creation: The Nuclear Crisis and a Just Peace.* This is the Council's response to the General Conference action (*The Book of Resolutions of The United Methodist Church 2004:* "Replace *In Defense of Creation* with new Document and Study Guide").

Aware of God's vision for creation, we no longer see a list of isolated problems affecting disconnected people, plants, and animals. Rather, we see one interconnected system that is "groaning in travail" (Romans 8:22 RSV). The threats to peace, people, and planet earth are related to one another, and God's vision encompasses complete well-being. We, your bishops, join with many global religious leaders to call for a comprehensive response to these interrelated issues. We urge all United Methodists and people of goodwill to offer themselves as instruments of God's renewing Spirit in the world.

We cannot be instruments of God's renewing Spirit in the world if we continue to deny the wounds of creation. Therefore, *let us join in a lament*[3] *for God's people and planet:*

Leader: We see waters polluted, species destroyed, forests ablaze, and land abused. We see weapons and waste littering the earth. We see people, created in the very image of God, suffering from famine and disease, burying their children, and living in hatred and fear. We know the farmers who cannot plant their fields because they are infested by land mines. We know the nations that build weapons of mass destruction and make plans to use them in the vain pursuit of security.
People: We lament the wounds on our beautiful planet.

Leader: We see people overwhelmed by fear and anxiety; people who find the wounds of the world too deep to address; people who see the challenges to health and well-being for all as too great to overcome. We know the workers who can no longer provide for their families and the activists exhausted by the struggle for justice.
People: We grieve for our world, filled with pain.

Leader: We see communities without basic health care and clean water; communities stripped of natural resources and denied access to land; communities torn apart by intolerance, religious extremism, and ethnic hatred. We know the refugee who risks death and capture searching for a safe place to live.
People: We weep for communities in crisis.

Leader: We see a world where some live opulently while others barely survive; a world where the innocent suffer and the corrupt profit; a world where too many still find their opportunities and freedom limited by skin color, gender, or birthplace. We know the boy who is caught in the snare of drugs and violence and the girl who is raped or forced into prostitution.
People: We mourn a world of inequality and injustice.

Leader: God sees the creation's wounds. God hears our lament. *And God calls us to accountability.* We cannot be instruments of God's renewal if we deny our complicity in pandemic poverty and disease, environmental degradation, and proliferation of weapons and violence.

Pastor: *We, the bishops of The United Methodist Church, confess our failure to lead our members to care for God's planet and people.* We do not always maintain the bond and balance between personal and social holiness that marks our Wesleyan heritage. We sometimes focus on internal church matters and neglect creation's daunting needs. We allow concerns about agreement and church growth to stifle our prophetic voice. We do not consistently provide the courageous leadership for peace and justice requested by our people. And too often we overlook expertise and gifts for leadership among our people.

We ask now that you join us in common confession, saying together:
All: As United Methodists, we confess our failure to embody the image of God. We rationalize our sin, satisfy our own desires, and exercise our freedom at the expense of the common good. We know that we should live within sustainable boundaries but we struggle to summon the moral will to change.[4] As individuals and communities of faith, we have not been the stewards and caretakers whom God created us to be.

Pastor: As your bishops, *we encourage you to find solace and strength in the knowledge that God's creative work continues.* This gracious and loving God still calls us forth and prepares us to care for one another and the planet. With John Wesley, let us all affirm the "unceasing presence of God, the loving, pardoning God, manifested to the heart, and perceived by faith," and turn to God offering "up all the thoughts of our hearts, all the words of our tongues, and all the works of our hands, all our body, soul, and spirit, to be an holy sacrifice, acceptable unto God in Christ Jesus."[5] We pray for the wisdom and courage to change the ways we live and work, relate to one another and the earth, and allow our nations to be governed. Through God's grace, we renew our minds, reorient our wills, and recommit ourselves to faithful discipleship as instruments of God's renewing Spirit. We rededicate ourselves faithfully to follow the One who came into the world to reconcile us to God and to one another.

In that spirit of rededication, we offer three general recommendations and nine particular pledges.

First, let us orient our lives toward God's holy vision. This vision of the future calls us to hope and to action. "For surely I know the plans I have for you, says the LORD, plans for your welfare and not for harm, to give you a future with hope" (Jeremiah 29:11). Christ's resurrection assures us that this vision is indeed a promise of renewal and reconciliation. As disciples of Christ, we take God's promise as the purpose for our lives. Let us, then, rededicate ourselves to God's holy vision, living each day with awareness of the future God extends to us and of the Spirit that leads us onward.

Second, let us practice social and environmental holiness. We believe personal holiness and social holiness must never be separated. John Wesley preached: "The gospel of Christ knows of no religion, but social. No holiness but social holiness."[6] Through social holiness we make ourselves channels of God's blessing in the world. Because God's blessing, care, and promise of renewal extend to all of creation, we can speak today of "environmental holiness" as well. We practice social and environmental holiness by caring for God's people and God's planet and by challenging those whose policies and practices neglect the poor, exploit the weak, hasten global warming, and produce more weapons.

Third, let us live and act in hope. As people in the tradition of John Wesley, we understand reconciliation and renewal to be part of the process of salvation that is already under way. We are not hemmed in to a fallen world. Rather, we are part of a divine, unfolding process to which we must contribute. As we faithfully respond to God's grace and call to action, the Holy Spirit guides us in this renewal. With a resurrection spirit, we look forward to the renewal of the whole creation and commit ourselves to that vision. We pray that God will accept and use our lives and resources that we rededicate to a ministry of peace, justice, and hope to overcome poverty and disease, environmental degradation, and the proliferation of weapons and violence.

With God's help and with you as our witnesses—

1. *We as your bishops pledge to answer God's call to deepen our spiritual consciousness as just stewards of creation.* We commit ourselves to faithful and effective leadership on these issues, in our denomination, and in our communities and nations.

2. *We pledge to make God's vision of renewal our goal.* With every evaluation and decision, we will ask: Does this contribute to God's renewal of creation? Ever aware of the difference between what is and what must be, we pledge to practice Wesleyan "holy dissatisfaction."[7]

3. *We pledge to practice dialogue with those whose life experience differs dramatically from our own, and we pledge to practice prayerful self-examination.* For example, in the Council of Bishops, the fifty active bishops in the United States are committed to listening and learning with the nineteen active bishops in Africa, Asia, and Europe. And the bishops representing conferences in the United States will prayerfully examine the fact that their nation consumes more than its fair share of the world's resources, generates the most waste, and produces the most weapons.

4. *We pledge ourselves to make common cause with religious leaders and people of good will worldwide who share these concerns.* We will connect and collaborate with ecumenical and interreligious partners and with community and faith organizations so that we may strengthen our common efforts.

5. *We pledge to advocate for justice and peace in the halls of power in our respective nations and international organizations.*

6. *We pledge to measure the "carbon footprint"[8] of our episcopal and denominational offices, determine how to reduce it, and implement those changes.* We will urge our congregations, schools, and settings of ministry to do the same.

7. *We pledge to provide, to the best of our ability, the resources needed by our conferences to reduce dramatically our collective exploitation of the planet, peoples, and communities, including technical assistance with buildings and programs, education and training, and young people's and online networking resources.*

8. *We pledge to practice hope as we engage and continue supporting the many transforming ministries of our denomination.* Every day we will thank God for fruit

produced through the work of The United Methodist Church and through each of you.

9. *We pledge more effective use of the Church and community Web pages to inspire and share what we learn.*[9] We celebrate the communications efforts that tell the stories of struggle and transformation within our denomination.

With these pledges, we respond to God's gracious invitation to join in the process of renewal. God is already visibly at work in people and groups around the world. We rededicate ourselves to join these movements, the movements of the Spirit. Young people are passionately raising funds to provide mosquito nets for their "siblings" thousands of miles away. Dockworkers are refusing to off-load small weapons being smuggled to armed combatants in civil wars in their continent. People of faith are demanding land reform on behalf of landless farm workers. Children and young people have formed church-wide "green teams" to transform our buildings and ministries into testimonies of stewardship and sustainability. Ecumenical and interreligious partners persist in demanding that the major nuclear powers reduce their arsenals, step by verifiable step, making a way to a more secure world totally disarmed of nuclear weapons. God is already doing a new thing. With this Letter and the accompanying Foundation Document, we rededicate ourselves to participate in God's work, and we urge you all to rededicate yourselves as well.

We beseech every United Methodist, every congregation, and every public leader: "Will you participate in God's renewing work?" We are filled with hope for what God can accomplish through us, and we pray you respond after each question: "We will, with God's help!"

Leader: Will you live and act in hope?
People: We will, with God's help.

Leader: Will you practice social and environmental holiness?
People: We will, with God's help.

Leader: Will you learn from one another and prayerfully examine your lives?
People: We will, with God's help.

Leader: Will you order your lives toward God's holy vision of renewal?
People: We will, with God's help.

Leader: With God's good creation imperiled by poverty and disease, environmental degradation, and weapons and violence, will you offer yourselves as instruments of God's renewing work in the world?
People: We will, with God's help.

Pastor: May God's grace purify our reason, strengthen our will, and guide our action. May the love of God, the peace of Christ, and the power of the Holy Spirit be among you, everywhere and always, so that you may be a blessing to all creation and to all the children of God, making peace, nurturing and practicing hope, choosing life, and coming to life eternal. Amen.

Notes

1. In 2002, the Reverend Dr. William Sloane Coffin, referring to a trio of political threats, said, "A more likely and far more dangerous trio would be environmental degradation, pandemic poverty, and a world awash with weapons" (*The Chautauqua Appeal*, with Joan Brown Campbell and Stephen J. Sidorak Jr.).

2. Unless otherwise noted, all scripture quotations are from the New Revised Standard Version of the Bible, copyright 1989, Division of Christian Education of the National Council of the Churches of Christ in the USA. Used by permission. All rights reserved. Quotations noted RSV are from the Revised Standard Version of the Bible, copyright 1952 [2nd edition, 1971] by the Division of Christian Education of the National Council of the Churches of Christ in the United States of America. Used by permission. All rights reserved.

3. This lament is offered as a responsive reading. The "pastor" is the voice of the bishops throughout the letter; the "leader" is another person who directs the lament; and the "people" are all those gathered together.

4. From *Hope in God's Future*, a report of the British Methodist Church Conference on *Christian Discipleship in the Context of Climate Change*, July 2009, Wolverhampton, UK.

5. John Wesley, Sermon 19: "The Great Privilege of Those That Are Born of God," *Works* 1:442.

6. *Hymns and Sacred Poems*, 1739, ¶5.

7. "When . . . Christian perfection becomes the goal, a fundamental hope is aroused that the future can surpass the present. And a corresponding holy dissatisfaction is aroused with regard to any present state of affairs—a dissatisfaction that supplies the critical edge necessary to keep the process of individual transformation moving. Moreover, this holy dissatisfaction is readily transferable from the realm of the individual to that of society, where it provides a persistent motivation for reform in the light of 'a more perfect way' that goes beyond any status quo." (Theodore Runyon, *The New Creation: John Wesley's Theology Today* [Nashville: Abingdon Press, 1998], p. 168.)

8. A "carbon footprint" is an estimate of how much carbon dioxide (a greenhouse gas) is produced to support life activities, including travel and home energy use. Carbon footprints are also applied on a larger scale to companies, businesses, and nations.

9. In support of the many persons who have followed this project of the Council, an interactive multimedia website will have resources, educational materials, downloadable video clips and social networking: www.hopeandaction.org

God's Renewed Creation: Call to Hope and Action

The Foundation Document*

Preface

More than twenty years ago (May 1986), after two years of prayerful study and consultation with specialists in many related fields, the United Methodist Council of Bishops offered a Pastoral Letter and a study document called *In Defense of Creation: The Nuclear Crisis and a Just Peace.*[1] It was an urgent message to all United Methodists and the Church at large on the growing threat of nuclear war and of the extinction of life on the planet through a "nuclear winter." It was an urgent reminder that this world belongs to God, "precious precisely because it is not our creation."[2] And it declared a "clear and unconditioned 'No' to nuclear war and to any use of nuclear weapons."[3] The documents received wide attention in the media, were translated into several languages, and were debated among leaders in the nuclear establishment. The Pastoral Letter was read aloud or published in newsletters in an estimated 90 percent of our congregations, supported by the Foundation Document and the guide for study and action. The following General Conference affirmed the document as the policy of The United Methodist Church.

In 2004, the General Conference of The United Methodist Church authorized the Council of Bishops to revisit these documents by "educating and encouraging the church, citizens and governments to seek things which lead to peace."[4] The result of this process is a new Pastoral Letter and Foundation Document, *God's Renewed Creation*, which is supplemented by study guides and a variety of Web-based materials. *God's Renewed Creation* maintains the firm commitment of the 1986 Council that "nuclear deterrence is a position that cannot receive the church's blessing." These documents, generated in 2009, also build on the observations of the earlier Council that the nuclear crisis threatens "planet earth itself," that the arms race "destroys millions of lives in conventional wars, repressive violence, and massive poverty," and that the "arms race is a social justice issue, not only a war and peace issue."[5] After many decades and millions of dollars, we are no more secure or peaceful in our world with a larger number of nations in the "nuclear club."

Today's nuclear peril is part of a complex "web of brokenness" that people of faith and goodwill must confront. The 2009 Council of Bishops expanded its focus to include three interrelated threats:

- pandemic poverty and disease,
- environmental degradation and climate change, and
- a world awash with weapons and violence.[6]

---

*Foundation Document, adopted November 3, 2009, at Lake Junaluska, N.C., U.S.A.

While we are not experts on these global issues, we are experts on the moral and ethical life that strengthens and supports God's intentions for Creation. As a strong and diverse global denomination, we speak as pastors to the Church and people of goodwill around our world calling for awareness, study, and action birthed of hope rather than fear.

The development of *God's Renewed Creation* reflects the purpose of The United Methodist Church to "make disciples of Jesus Christ for the transformation of the world." We know the world is being transformed and we seek to cooperate with God's renewing Spirit, especially through our denomination's Four Areas of Focus: (1) developing principled Christian leaders for the church and the world, (2) creating new places for new people and renewing existing congregations, (3) engaging in ministry with the poor, and (4) stamping out the killer diseases of poverty. Focusing on these four areas will shape our discipleship such that those who seek God will see an image in our behavior that is inviting, encouraging, healing, and inspiring. This project, *God's Renewed Creation*, furthers these goals.

God's Renewed Creation is a rallying voice and a demonstration of rededicated leadership by the bishops to engage, inspire, and rouse United Methodists and people of goodwill to a deeper spiritual consciousness as stewards and caretakers of Creation. These documents remind us all of the possibility and promise of hope and God's renewal. They challenge us to ask "What now shall we do?" to be true disciples of Jesus Christ to address this web of threats. *God's Renewed Creation* also provides recommendations and guidelines for answering this question of discipleship.

Moreover, these documents create space for individuals, congregations, and ecumenical and interreligious bodies to discern and implement their own responses, given their particular context. As bishops serving a global church, we know that our people have different kinds of experiences with the problems of poverty and disease, environmental degradation, and weapons and violence. We prioritize these problems differently and have varying levels of power and resources for addressing them. However, we also insist that these issues *pose a common threat to our shared future*. We must treat them as interrelated issues, and we must work together, each of us contributing what we can, to eradicate poverty and disease, stop the destruction of our natural world, and reverse our reliance on weapons and violence.

Through the Pastoral Letter and Foundation Document, we share our hope and expectations for our United Methodist Church, and describe the power and influence we can bring if we work in concerted, international, and ecumenical/ interreligious action. Included at the Web site www.hopeandaction.org are lists of resources, other valuable online networks, and key Resolutions from *The United Methodist Book of Resolutions* that are rich in action ideas and educational materials. Also included are a timeline for the studies, a guide for action planning in congregations and conferences, and ways to stay connected to share stories of struggle, progress, and hope. Receive this with our prayers that God will be merciful and sustain us with responsible hope as we go forward.

❖ ❖ ❖

God's Renewed Creation: Call to Hope and Action

For many hundreds of years "the People of the Book"—Jews, Christians, and Muslims—have lived through hard times of drought, fire, floods, raging waters, and tempestuous winds, sustained by the ancient wisdom of the psalmists, who over and over again sang of "the steadfast love of the Lord."

Today, the human family is awakening to alarming news: after several thousand years of a stable climate that enabled us to thrive, the earth is heating up at an accelerating rate. Climate change poses a particular threat to the world's poor because it increases the spread of diseases like malaria and causes conflicts over dwindling natural resources. Easy access to small arms ensures that such conflicts turn deadly, and the specter of a nuclear war that would destroy the earth continues to loom over us.

Clearly we have arrived at a hinge of history, a revolutionary time of great challenge. We turn again to the ancient wisdom and remember the ringing challenge of God: "Behold, I am doing a new thing; / now it springs forth, do you not perceive it?" (Isaiah 43:19 RSV). Do we not see signs that God is at work in this crisis?

As the earth is being transformed, God has blessed human beings with the capacity to read the signs of the times and to respond with intelligence and faith. Learned scientists and experts monitor the changes that have an impact on our very survival. They are clarifying the measures we must take immediately to save our forests, oceans, air, and human and animal ecosystems.

More than that, God has inspired human beings to envision new futures and to invent the tools necessary to make them a reality: technologies to replace fossil fuels with energy from the wind and sun; new forms of transportation; "green jobs"; and guides for cutting carbon footprints. Thousands and thousands of persons in faith-based and community-based coalitions, congregations, businesses, and farms are already acting for change in quiet, persistent, and profound ways.

Even further, God is bringing people together to plan and to act upon emerging realities: villages, towns, and local governments urge and guide neighbors to share common causes; cities, states, and nations identify the special needs of their citizens and implement solutions; the United Nations and international agencies research global problems, identify solutions, and shape the organizations to address them. Public leaders are working at a feverish pace to reshape the rules of engagement between humans and the earth. Empowering all these efforts is an amazing network of globe-circling monetary, industrial, transportation, and communications systems such as the human family has never before known.

Finally, Christian and interreligious communities are speaking out boldly on the interrelated nature of the present crisis. For example, the *Ecumenical Declaration on Just Peace* currently being drafted by the World Council of Churches names justice, peace, and the integrity of creation.

Why is all of this activity happening? Because the peoples of the world are reading the signs carefully—we see clearly that God is doing a new thing, and that God is inviting the human family to participate in transformation.

Called to Speak a Word of Hope and Action

In 2004, the General Conference of The United Methodist Church took an explicit step in this movement by calling on the Council of Bishops to offer a word of hope and a call to action in light of the triple threat to peace, people, and planet earth. This Foundation Document is one piece of our response, as your bishops, in addition to the Pastoral Letter, study guides, and a number of Web-based resources. This Foundation Document:

- describes the interconnected nature of poverty and disease, environmental degradation, and weapons and violence through stories of those most affected;
- shares information about Christian scriptures and beliefs and our Wesleyan heritage in order to provide a foundation for our response;
- recommends a variety of actions; and
- reminds us of the guidance of the Holy Spirit and the great sources of encouragement and hope all around us.

Listening with Open Minds and Hearts

Over the past two years, the bishops have asked United Methodists in every region of our denomination—Africa, Asia, Europe, and the United States—as well as interreligious and ecumenical colleagues about their concerns, their own responses to the crises, and what they hoped to hear in the Pastoral Letter and this Foundation Document. The most persistent requests were that the bishops:

- speak to the fear, anxiety, frustration, and concern for future generations;
- lead a confession of our greed and selfishness;
- offer a reminder of our biblical and theological grounding, and Wesleyan passion for social holiness;
- call for transformation of lifestyles, systems, and structures;
- give special attention to the sense of urgency, impatience, and cynicism felt by our young people;
- as bishops, exemplify living and working in sustainable communities;
- suggest what we can do in prayer, study, and action; and
- guide our turn from fear and concern to hope and action.

This Foundation Document supplements the Pastoral Letter by serving as a reference for prayerful reflection, study, and action. It puts real stories and faces on victims of unjust systems and structures. It describes the context of ministry as we plan and connect with others. It helps prepare us spiritually and mentally to be instruments of God's renewing work. "God's Renewed Creation" moves us all out of isolation and fear and into the streets of our communities and our world with hope and promise because *we cannot help the world until we change our own way of being in it.*

An Honest Look at Our Situation

We must prepare our hearts and minds by turning to God and placing all anxiety, loss, and grief before the One who is our ever-present help in time of trouble. And, with God's grace, we remember the story that guides and sustains us, holds us accountable, and gives us hope. It is the story that begins with God's loving gift of creation and culminates in God's promise of renewal for all. It is the story of the Word made flesh, the Incarnation, God's presence with us. It is the story of Jesus' ministry to the most vulnerable, his denunciation of violence, greed, and oppression, and his call to discipleship. It is the story of resurrection, of the triumph of life over death, and of the promise of new life in Christ. And it is the story of transformation, from old to new, from woundedness to wholeness, and from injustice and violence to the embrace of righteousness and peace.

We have a role to play in this story, but we have not faithfully performed it. God entrusted us with creation. But, instead of faithfully caring for our peaceful planet and its people, we have neglected the poor, polluted our air and water, and filled our communities with instruments of war. We have turned our backs on God and one another. By obstructing God's will, we have contributed to pandemic poverty and disease, environmental degradation, and the proliferation of weapons and violence.[7] Around the world, we feel the effects of this interconnected trio in different ways and to varying degrees, but there is no doubt that we all are experiencing elements of the same storm.

The storm builds as powerful forces swirl together:

To affect poverty: The **global economic crisis** as systems built upon self-interest and fraud devastate the global economy; the **resource crisis** as food, water, and energy become scarce; the **justice/poverty crisis** as the gap between rich and poor continues to widen; the **global health crisis** as millions die of the preventable diseases of poverty like malaria, HIV/AIDS, and tuberculosis; and the **refugee crisis** as millions of people are displaced by violence, natural disaster, and loss of jobs.

To affect the environment: The **energy crisis** as oil reserves run out within two or three decades; the **climate crisis** as increasing greenhouse gases threaten to scorch the earth and the expansion of deserts erodes productive land, polar ice melts, fire seasons lengthen, and coastal floods and severe storms increase in number; the **biodiversity crisis** as at least one-fifth of all plant and animal species face extinction by 2050.

To affect weapons and violence: The **weapons crisis** as the threat of nuclear, biological, and chemical attack looms and precious resources are poured into the sinkhole of futile arms races[8]; the **small arms crisis** as roughly 639 million small arms and light weapons circulate the world and the illegal small arms trade is estimated at close to $1 billion[9]; the **"security" crisis** as global military spending surpasses 1.2 trillion USD in 2007, with the United States spending 45 percent of this amount.

Because these threats are interconnected, each one compounds the effects of the others. This means that people and the planet experience the cumulative effects of this storm. The interrelated nature of these threats also makes it exceedingly difficult to make any real headway on any individual issue. We find ourselves overwhelmed by complex *webs of brokenness*: injustice against migrants, resource scarcity elevated to warfare, energy crises, environmental racism, economic globalization, and violence against the most vulnerable, especially women and girls.

Lives Threatened by the Storm

Each person affected by this trio of threats has a story. These are just a few that we have heard.

• From the Philippines, we learned about seven-year-old Rosalie, who died on November 21, 2007. "She was among those who are suffering extreme hunger in Rapu-rapu, a fishing community in Albay, Bicol, a place that has been environmentally devastated, where sources of livelihood have been disrupted since the mining corporation started operation."[10] Rosalie died of hunger on her way home from school.

• Our bishops in Angola tell us about the landmines that make farmland unusable. The land simply lies fallow because farming it would be deadly, and removing the landmines is too expensive and dangerous. Angola is one of eighty-two countries affected by landmines manufactured in fifteen other countries. The most conservative estimate is that removing landmines costs one hundred times as much as making them. An estimated fifteen to twenty thousand people are hurt or killed by landmines every year.[11]

• In part of the Appalachian Mountains of the eastern United States, roughly one thousand metric tons of explosive are used every day to blast away the tops of mountains and ridges to reach coal seams underneath. Mountaintop removal (MTR) destroys animal and plant environments, causes landslides, floods, and toxic streams, and generates long-term threats to health and safety. At current rates, MTR will mine over 1.4 million acres in the United States by 2010. This is an area larger than the state of Delaware, USA.[12]

God's Promise and Our Purpose

For surely I know the plans I have for you, says the LORD,
plans for your welfare and not for harm, to give you a future with hope.
(Jeremiah 29:11)

It is understandable that looking out on this broken and suffering world would cause despair. But the brokenness and suffering are not the complete story. They are part of our experience, but not the sum total of it. Amidst corruption, there is honesty; amidst greed, there is generosity; amidst killing, there is compassion; amidst destruction, there is creation; amidst devastation, there is preservation; amidst apathy, there is righteous indignation, holy dissatisfaction, and a passion for the possible. If we look carefully, we see seeds of hope that can be cultivated by God's Spirit.

• In East Africa, dockworkers refused to off-load a foreign vessel carrying smuggled small arms. Doing what they could to stop the killing in their continent, they also sent word to other dockworkers to refuse the shipment when it arrived farther south.

• United Methodists from Lage, Germany, forged a partnership with people in Cambine, Mozambique, to promote solar energy. They installed solar panels on the local maternity hospital and a theological seminary. The first boy born in the maternity ward after solar light was installed was named "Solarino" to celebrate the renewable energies bringing new life to God's creation.

• In a number of U.S. cities, people of faith are working to end the "straw purchase" of handguns—guns that are purchased legally but then passed into the hands of those who could not legally buy for themselves. Nonviolent volunteers with Heeding God's Call raise awareness; they approach gun retailers directly and ask them to accept responsibility for the role they play in violence and to voluntarily end this destructive practice.

• Since fourteen people were killed during a workers' strike in 2004 in the Philippines, members of The United Methodist Church and ecumenical groups of adults and young people have organized weekly to visit workers, hear their stories, witness struggles, visit the Congress, circulate petitions, and renew their resolve to work for justice and peace. These life-changing experiences of sharing strengths, fears, and vulnerability, as well as faith and love, empower young people to choose hope amidst discouragement.

Stories about our disregard for and destruction of one another and the earth more frequently grab the headlines. But acts of perseverance, compassion, care, and positive innovation take place every day in every corner of our world. Right now, there is someone writing a letter to oppose a discriminatory practice or to advocate on behalf of workers treated unjustly, or to support the ratification of a weapons ban. The United Methodist Committee on Relief is setting up disaster response centers and training to "prevent a bad thing from becoming worse."[13] Someone is sitting by a bedside to provide comfort. In a community center, a trainer prepares a group to use methods of nonviolent resistance in order to make a change without violence.

Somewhere, a new school is opening and a new well is functioning. People are unpacking boxes of medical supplies and mosquito nets. Children are educating their parents about global warming, and organizations are examining their carbon footprint. New forms of transportation are coming on the market: hybrid cars and plug-in cars and hydrogen cars and cleaner-burning diesels that do not give children respiratory diseases as they roar through neighborhoods. With the tools of ecumenical organizations, congregations are doing energy audits, recycling materials, replacing energy-guzzling appliances, and installing solar panels and wind turbines.

No matter how discouraging things seem, no matter how overwhelmed and anxious we feel, no matter how apathetic or cynical we become, God is already at work in the world. We must only *open our eyes* to see God's vision, *open our hearts* to receive God's grace, and *open our hands* to do the work God calls us to do.

We open our eyes to God's vision for this renewed Creation, to God's Spirit active in the world, and to our role as channels of God's blessing. When we open our eyes to God's vision, we no longer see a list of isolated problems affecting disconnected people, plants, and animals. Rather, we see one interconnected system that "has been groaning in travail" (Romans 8:22 RSV). We see that the threats to peace, people, and planet earth are related to one another, and that God's vision encompasses complete global health. When we open our eyes to God's vision of renewal, we also clearly see the ways in which we obstruct God's process. When we open our eyes to the presence of God's renewing Spirit in the world, we celebrate every charitable act, every just practice, every courageous stand for peace, every moment of reconciliation, every cessation of violence, and every restored habitat as a glimpse of the Kingdom of God, as a "seed-like presence of that which is hoped for."[14]

We might think of opening our eyes as a spiritual discipline rooted in John Wesley's understanding of the "natural image of God" (*Works* 2:188).[15] Three gifts are included in the basic equipment our Creator has given us as spiritual beings to be both independent and at the same time to relate to God and our neighbor. The first of these gifts is *reason*—the human ability to discern order and relationships, to grasp how things work, and to make judgments. The second gift is our *will*—the ability to commit ourselves to God, to persons, and to goals, and to carry through. The third gift is our *freedom*. God does not want automatons. "A mere machine" is not morally answerable, says Wesley. Human responsibility requires freedom (*Works* [Jackson] 10:234).

Therefore, we reflect the natural image of God when we exercise our reason for accurate understanding and good judgment, and when we respond to God's grace by freely exercising our will to choose good and resist evil. We open our eyes in order to perceive the world accurately, understand our roles and responsibilities, and exercise good judgment.

We open our hearts to confess our sin, to receive God's grace, to discern God's call, and to feel strengthened by God's sustaining Spirit. We are not initiating these actions; rather we are responding to God's gracious invitation to join God's renewal of creation. God invites us, with all of our imperfections, to participate in this work. We open our hearts so that we can change. We open our hearts to feel God's presence with us as we labor. We open our hearts "that we may anchor our souls in the One who is just, who renews our strength for the work to be done."[16]

We open our hearts to embody the "moral image of God," to use Wesley's words (*Works* 2:188). This moral image is not something we possess but is ours only insofar as we continually receive it from the Source. We embody the moral image of God as we receive God's grace and then reflect that grace out into the world. To describe this process of receiving and reflecting God's grace, Wesley used the image of breath, calling it "spiritual respiration": "God's breathing into the soul, and the soul's breathing back what it first receives from God; a continual *action* of God upon the soul, the *re-action* of the soul upon God" (*Works* 1:442).

We open our hands to respond to the Spirit and do the work God calls us to do in the world. As human beings created in God's image, we have a special responsibility to care for the gift of creation. Wesley calls this "the political image of God" (*Works* 2:188). We often live as though "being created in God's image" gives us special privilege, but living with that assumption is a grave mistake. Our status as human beings increases our *responsibility*, not our *privilege*. Being created in God's image means that we are charged with caring for this world, not invited to abuse it.[17] Doing justice, building peace, and mending the planet are ways that we take care of what we have been given. However, we are not caretakers for an absentee landlord; rather, God's renewing Spirit works through us and courses around us, breathing new life into the planet and its people.

"We are now God's stewards," says Wesley. "We are indebted to God for all that we have. . . . A steward is not at liberty to use what is lodged in his hands as he pleases, but as his master pleases. . . . He is not the owner of any of these things but barely entrusted with them by another" (*Works* 2:283). The care of the earth is entrusted to us. We are the "channels of God's blessings to the other creatures and to the earth itself" (*Works* 2:440).

With Open Eyes, We See God's Vision

With open eyes, we see God's vision for the whole of creation. Our Christian understanding of the Kingdom of God is deeply informed by the Hebrew prophetic tradition that formed Jesus. This is why we often think of Isaiah's prophecy as a description of the Kingdom of God:

> No more shall be heard the sound of weeping in [Jerusalem],
> > or the cry of distress.
> No more shall there be in it
> > an infant that lives but a few days
> > or an old person who does not live out a lifetime. . . .
> They shall build houses and inhabit them;
> > they shall plant vineyards and eat their fruit. . . .
> They shall not labor in vain,
> > or bear children for calamity. (Isaiah 65:19b, 20a, 21, 23a)

This is an inclusive vision of well-being. People and the land are healthy and safe. It is the vision of Shalom, which includes "living in harmony and security toward the joy and well-being of every other creature."[18] It is a vision of wholeness.

In his Letter to the Romans, Paul gives us a vision of glory that extends to all of creation. "We know that the whole creation has been groaning in travail together until now," he writes. But "the creation itself will be set free from its bondage to decay and obtain the glorious liberty of the children of God" (Romans 8:22, 21 RSV). God has not only offered the gift of creation, but also promises its renewal.

When preaching on this text, John Wesley underscored its meaning for "brute creation." "While [God's] creatures 'travail together in pain,' [God] knoweth all their pain." He continues, "In the new earth, as well as in the new heavens, there will be nothing to give pain, but everything that the wisdom and goodness of God can create to give happiness." God's promise of salvation is extended to the whole of creation, not just human beings (*Works* 2:445). God's work of salvation has cosmic proportions.

In Colossians, we read that the reconciling and unifying work of Christ extends to all of creation as well. As "the firstborn of all creation," Christ "is before all things, and in him all things hold together." "For in him all the fullness of God was pleased to dwell, and through him God was pleased to reconcile to himself all things, whether on earth or in heaven" (Colossians 1:15, 17, 19-20). The resurrection thus serves as "the pledge or promise of the full redemption to come."[19] The renewal of creation is God's promise.

The gospel writers often describe Jesus as "preaching the gospel of the kingdom and healing every disease and every infirmity among the people" (Matthew 4:23 RSV). Healing and preaching the Kingdom of God were part of the same ministry for Jesus. This process of preparing for the Kingdom of God, of renewing creation, is akin to a healing process. God is healing the planet.

John Wesley held firmly to this language of healing in his own preaching and teaching. Indeed, one of his favorite metaphors for God was "the Great Physician" (*Works* 2:184). For Wesley, God is fundamentally concerned about well-being. Salvation is understood holistically, as complete holiness and happiness. When we expand that notion of salvation to the planet, we see that God's work of renewing creation is comprehensive. In the hands of the Great Physician, every aspect of our world is being made whole or healthy. Poverty and disease, environmental degradation, and violence are signs of our ill health. God is working toward the health of the whole body. If we are to fashion ourselves as instruments of God's renewing work in the world, we too must direct our efforts toward healing our collective body.

With Open Eyes, We See Relationships

With open eyes, we see the relationships between poverty and disease, environmental degradation, and the proliferation of weapons and violence. Although this makes the problems seem even more difficult to surmount, treating them separately is less effective. To accurately diagnose our situation and craft a viable plan for health, we must see and respond to the ways in which the particular threats interact with one another. For example, we cannot address global poverty without addressing water shortage made worse every day by global warming. We cannot stem the proliferation of weapons without examining dwindling natural resources or minerals as causes of violent conflict. We cannot talk about the need for health care, schools, roads, and wells without re-evaluating the amount of money we spend on weapons.

Although we may prioritize poverty and disease, environmental degradation, and weapons differently in light of our individual experiences, we must not lose sight of the connections among them. And we must reject policies and practices that pit the victims of these problems against one another. We must see these problems as linked, like three connected rings, so that a solution for one improves the situation for the others.

In its "Minute on Global Warming and Climate Change," the World Council of Churches captures the relationship between environmental degradation, poverty, and disease:

> Those who are and will increasingly be affected [by climate change] are the impoverished and vulnerable communities of the global South who are much more dependent on natural resources for their subsistence and do not have the means to

adapt to the changes. Deforestation in Africa, Asia and Latin America; the increase in vector-borne diseases (like dengue or malaria) in the higher altitude areas of Africa as a result of the increase in temperature; the forced migration, displacement and resettlement of populations as a result of sea level rise, particularly in the Pacific, are some of the impacts that will continue to increase the pressure on poor and vulnerable communities.[20]

Citing the 2007 report of the Intergovernmental Panel on Climate Change, the Evangelical Environmental Network tells us that "40–170 million additional poor people could be at risk of hunger and malnutrition in this century" due to the decrease in agricultural output. "One to two billion people already in a water-stressed situation could see a further reduction in water availability."[21]

Many global partners have been hard at work on the United Nations Millennium Development Goals—goals to lift the extreme poor of the world by addressing the interconnected issues of severe poverty, disease, sustainable development, globalization, education, and human rights. But the fight will not be won easily.

> Seeing through the lens of the poor and hungry . . . we see how a multiplicity of crises—of food, fuel and finance—have grossly disadvantaged the very beneficiaries of the Goals. We cannot assume that the myriad of crises we experience daily—food crisis, financial crisis, energy crisis, climate crisis—are going to be solved by policy makers, let alone the very people and forces that have led us into the brink of these crises.[22]

Diverting resources toward the manufacture and purchase of weapons also worsens poverty. We have known this for a long time. U.S. President Eisenhower said in 1953, "Every gun that is made, every warship launched, every rocket fired is, in a sense, a theft from those who hunger and are not fed, those who are cold and are not clothed."[23]

We also see that the world's poor—especially women, children, elders, and persons of racial and ethnic minority—bear the burden of dwindling natural resources and quite literally "get dumped on" by those who export their waste. We know that the poor and powerless are stuck with polluted land and water while others move on to "greener pastures." And for many communities, "going green" has a short-term expense that pushes the long-term benefits out of reach for the poor. Therefore, "we cannot separate the plight of the poor from the plight of the planet. . . . Those least responsible for creating this problem are most vulnerable to its effects."[24]

Around the world, dwindling or otherwise valuable natural resources fuel violent conflict. In the Democratic Republic of Congo, for example, militias are raping women, abducting children to be soldiers or sex slaves, and burning villages in their fight to control mineral-rich land. In other cases, land is not necessarily a cause of conflict, but it becomes a consequence. Farmlands littered with land mines are just one example. An age-old practice in warfare is the purposeful destruction of the land so that communities are completely displaced.

While conventional weapons are already damaging creation piece by piece, nuclear weapons "could transform the planet and all its inhabitants into a dreary waste of ash and cinder."[25] Moreover, as a global community, we have yet to solve the life-threatening dilemma of the safe disposal of nuclear waste. Our geopolitical situation has changed dramatically since the Cold War, but as U.S. President Barack Obama recently stated, "The threat of global nuclear war has gone down, but the risk of a nuclear attack has gone up."[26] And two critical years have passed since a team of four "Cold War patriarchs" urgently called for the elimination of nuclear weapons entirely, including a reinvigorated commitment to the Non-Proliferation Treaty eliminating all nuclear arsenals of the nuclear powers, ratification of the Comprehensive Test Ban Treaty banning all nuclear explosions, and a joint international effort to eliminate all nuclear arms, step by verifiable step.[27]

When we see all of creation as one body, we know that our collective health cannot be realized as long as some still suffer. Forty years ago from his cell in the Birmingham jail, the Reverend Dr. Martin Luther King, Jr. penned his famous line: "Injustice anywhere is a threat to justice everywhere." Written during the economic crisis in 2009, *A Message to the People of The United Methodist Church* reads, "We are no more secure than the most vulnerable among us; no more prosperous than the poorest; and no more assured of justice and dignity than those who live in the shadows of power, void of fairness and equity."[28] As disciples of Christ, who show special concern for the most vulnerable members of society, *we must open our eyes to the ways in which environmental degradation and violence particularly hurt the poor and marginalized.*

Poverty, environmental degradation, and violence form a lethal combination that threatens all of creation; but they pose a more severe risk to societies and communities inhabited by people of color. Across Europe and the Americas, racial and ethnic minority communities bear the brunt of harmful pollutants from factories, laboratories, and nuclear power plants; dumping of poisonous wastes; mining the earth for fossil fuels; and the replacing or severing of neighborhoods by highways and commercial buildings.

For example, for decades Native American tribes and reservations throughout the Western United States have faced the gravest danger from public and private efforts to mine uranium and transport and store nuclear waste and radioactive materials on their lands. Much of the hazardous wastes targeted to these lands are left over from production of weapons for war. Members and allies of the Western Shoshone people are still fighting U.S. government efforts to bury atomic waste at Yucca Mountain in Nevada, a sacred site for the tribe. When tribal leader Ian Zabarte accused U.S. officials of "environmental racism" at a 2007 public hearing, the room erupted in applause, demonstrating the pain and anger many Native people feel about this potentially lethal pollution of their land and water resources. Indigenous peoples have much to teach the world from their wisdom about the earth and the consequences of defiling it.[29]

It is women who suffer most from poverty and disease, environmental degradation, and weapons and violence. About 70 percent of the world's poor are women and children, many living in areas where housing is marginal and daily living strenuous. Because of this, women and children pay a hefty price when caught in natural disasters exacerbated by climate change.[30] Women traditionally shoulder the burden of household food production both in Africa and Asia, while men may tend to focus on growing cash crops or migrate to cities to find paid work. Yet women own a tiny percentage of the world's farmland—some say as little as 1 percent. [31]

Civil conflict and environmental degradation make it more difficult and even deadly for women to meet the daily needs of their families. Every day, women are subjected to rape and other forms of violence while they search for firewood and fetch clean water. Rape and sexual slavery are instruments of war such that women and girls in conflict zones experience multiple forms of violence. [32] Worldwide, one out of three women experiences some level of abuse in her life. [33] And, in too many places, women are denied power in decision-making processes regarding the issues that affect their well-being so profoundly. Women and children are indeed the most vulnerable in our global family.

With Open Hearts, We Acknowledge Our Complicity

In our discussion "The World Community" in the Social Principles of The United Methodist Church, we acknowledge this fact: "Some nations possess more military and economic power than do others" (¶165.B). Some nations consume more of the world's resources, generate more of the world's waste, and produce more of the world's weapons. For example:

• Twenty percent of the world's population accounts for 76 percent of private consumption of things like electricity, paper, meat and fish, and vehicle usage.[34]

• "A mere 12% of the world's population uses 85% of its water, and these 12% do not live in the Third World."[35]

• The United States is the largest supplier of conventional weapons in the world, selling 38 percent of all weapons purchased between 2000 and 2007—roughly one-half of these weapons were sold or transferred to developing countries.[36]

There are many ways to designate the differences between us: Global North and Global South; first world and third world; first world and two-thirds world; developed world and developing world. We must also acknowledge that there is deep poverty and underdevelopment in the so-called first world, and there are pockets of wealth and opulence in the so-called third world.

Our social and economic situations are much more complex than any labels or statistics can capture. And yet, some generalizations are also true and important. Those of us in the Global North consume more, waste more, and militarize more than those of us in the Global South. We in the North must take responsibility for the environmental damage we have caused, what many now call our "environmental or ecological debt."[37] We must reckon with our vain pursuit of security through weapons and violence.[38] We must also confess the greed and selfishness that motivate us to pursue our own comfort while ignoring those in need.

We also recognize that "no nation or culture is absolutely just and right in its treatment of its own people."[39] We in the Global South must acknowledge corruption that threatens our societies. Like our brothers and sisters in the North, we too must challenge our nations' quest for security through weaponry. When we spend precious resources on weapons, we are stealing from the poor of our country. We confess selfishness and greed, made worse in contexts of scarcity.

We join together in acknowledging that we have resources and gifts that we hide under bushel baskets (Matthew 5:15) instead of utilizing them for the glory of God and to the benefit of God's good earth. We have opportunities for charity and justice-making that we do not exercise. We have also failed to encourage the gifts and energies of our young people by not involving them in community building, leadership, and development. And we have not done enough to stop violence against women and children. At times we all fall prey to despair, losing sight of God's presence with us and failing to hear God's call to us. We ask for God's help and grace as we turn away from harmful practices and commit ourselves to God's purpose of renewal for all.

With open hearts, we pray:
Make us wise as to how fragile and dependent and connected we are,
that in the indulgence in the destruction of others,
we inevitably destroy ourselves.
Give us the grace to be thankful for what we have,
and the willingness to share.
As your church labours in the world,
cause it to be more interested
in your reign of righteousness
than in its own survival,
so that the world may grow into a kinder, gentler, safer place
in which to live.[40]

With Open Hearts, We Respond to God's Grace

We cannot rely on our own sense of purpose and strength for this work of renewal. Rather, we absolutely require "transcendent resources." We turn to God to inform, infuse, and inspire us. We seek "partnership with and participation in the divine Spirit." However, "*humanity* cannot on its own initiate this relationship. We cannot produce the covenant [with the Creator], for the initiative must come from the other side. . . . And the name for this initiative from the other side is *grace*."[41]

John Wesley understood grace to be "God's love for humanity made evident in Christ." When we open our hearts to receive this grace, forgiveness and renewal become possible.[42] However, renewal in our personhood is incomplete. Breathing in the grace of God is the first step; we must also breathe God's grace out into the world. In doing so, we become a channel of God's blessing. We experience synergy (working together) between God's grace and our human response. We move toward restoring the image of God in humanity and contributing to the renewal of creation.

God's Renewed Creation: Call to Hope and Action

And we celebrate the presence of the Holy Spirit, which is "called 'holy' [precisely] because it sanctifies life and renews the face of the earth."[43]

With Open Hands, We Do the Work to Which God Calls Us

In order to live fully in God's image, we must make God's promise our purpose. We respond to the groaning of creation *and* to this vision of renewal by making ourselves a channel of God's blessing. We open our hearts to receive God's grace, and we open our hands in response, to do the work God calls us to do. What does it really mean to fashion ourselves as instruments of God's renewing Spirit? This is not a new question. It is, in fact, a variation of the question posed to Jesus many times: "What must I do to inherit eternal life?" (Luke 10:25). Jesus answers with the dual love commandment: " 'You shall love the Lord your God with all your heart, and with all your soul, and with all your mind.' This is the greatest and first commandment. And a second is like it: 'You shall love your neighbor as yourself' " (Matthew 22:37-39). Participating in God's work of renewal looks like love shining forth in action.

We love God by paying attention to God's creation. We pay attention to poverty, environmental degradation, and weapons and violence. Neglecting these ills and those who suffer their effects is contrary to love. We respond to Jesus' commandment by paying attention to our world. And we begin to fashion ourselves as instruments of God's renewal by deepening our spiritual consciousness as faithful stewards and directing our attention to the world God loves.[44]

We love God and neighbor by practicing compassionate respect.[45] We extend our care and concern, and provide assistance and comfort as needed. But we also respect the ones cared for as subjects in their own right. We respect the earth, knowing that it is not ours to plunder. We respect those suffering poverty and disease, granting them full autonomy to determine their own needs and path to well-being. We respect victims of violence by supporting their pursuit of a just peace. In sum, we "work toward societies in which each person's value is recognized, maintained, and strengthened."[46]

We love God and neighbor by changing our behavior. We cannot be instruments of love if we hold on to selfishness and greed. Jesus calls us to love, but he also calls us to conversion, to a radical change in our lifestyle and attitude. His message is clear: We cannot help the world until we change our own way of being in it.

We love God and neighbor by challenging those who do harm. We must not only respond to the suffering already created, but also challenge people, companies, and governments that continue to exploit the weak, destroy the earth, perpetuate violence, and generate more weapons. We follow Jesus' example of confronting authorities nonviolently, using the force of love.[47] And we adhere to our Social Principles, which affirm the "right of individuals to dissent when acting under the constraint of conscience."[48]

Anyone who has experienced genuine love knows its power. Looking at the world through the eyes of faith, we can see love at work, transforming an abandoned lot into a community garden, transforming a neglected child into a healthy and happy toddler, and transforming people at war into communities committed to reconciliation. We witness God's work of renewal in these pockets of transformation. And we participate in that work of renewal by living fully as Christ's disciples, people whose love of God and neighbor shines forth in action.

Call to Hope and Action

John Wesley insisted, "The gospel of Christ knows of no religion but social. No holiness but social holiness. Faith working by love is the length and breadth and depth and height of Christian perfection" (Preface to *Hymns and Sacred Poems*, 1739, ¶5). Ours is not solely a private faith, but one that also orients us toward God *and* the needs of our neighbor and world. At a time when people are cynical about religion, United Methodists must continue our rich heritage of "faith working by love" as an example of the church's ability to make a positive difference in the world.

The leaders and members of our denomination have a long tradition of speaking truth to power, naming injustice, and advocating for right relationships and equitable sharing among all God's peoples. Today, United Methodists protest racism and abuse directed toward illegal immigrants (as well as legal immigrants sometimes perceived to be illegal) and challenge local and federal authorities to maintain a democracy open to all people. In Arizona, Bishop Minerva Carcaño joins thousands in protest; and in Texas, United Methodist Women and the Board of Church and Society organize interreligious prayer vigils that include people from ten different countries.

We feel the energy in thousands of ministries every day in our United Methodist connection. We are strengthened and inspired by the Toberman Neighborhood House in San Pedro, California, which provides services for gang prevention and gang intervention, family counseling and mental health, child care, and community organizing. The Toberman House is one of a hundred national mission institutions founded by the women of the Methodist tradition; it was started in 1903 and is still supported by UMW Mission Giving.

Today, we are increasingly aware of the powerful role that young adults are playing to transform our societies and to challenge our church to live out its commitments to social justice, creation care, and peace. For example, every year, young adult interns with the Micah Corps in the Nebraska Annual Conference immerse themselves in social justice education, training, and advocacy on behalf of the poor and marginalized in their state.

During the many listening and learning events that informed the Pastoral Letter and Foundation Document, participants did much more than articulate their concern about poverty and disease, environmental degradation, and weapons and violence. From ages ten to one hundred, they expressed their deep desire to do something about these problems and their great hope that change is possible. These conversations raised awareness about several things:

1. We must study, observe, learn from, and listen to one another, especially to victims of these threats. Some of us are indeed aware of these problems, but less aware of the interconnections, and even less aware of our personal connections and complicity or the dramatic urgency in what is already

happening in our communities. We must listen with particular care to our young people, whose knowledge, consciousness, and impatience for action can be energizing and inspiring for us all.

2. We can be re-energized and spiritually renewed by the examples from our own Wesleyan and United Methodist heritage and experience. We belong to an amazing denomination with transforming potential already active and agile in thousands of ministry settings including legislatures, parliaments, and congresses.

3. We need an ongoing word of hope as we follow Wesley out into the streets and communities to face uncomfortable and difficult things and connect with others working for justice, peace, and the integrity of creation.[49]

4. "For God all things are possible" (Matthew 19:26). We have immense hope, and it will grow as we study, act, and connect.

As your bishops, we have taken to heart this desire to enable change, making several commitments and nine specific pledges in our Pastoral Letter. Here is our encouragement for all people of faith and goodwill to consider these calls to action.

Let Us Order Our Lives toward God's Holy Vision

- Renew our understandings of God's holy vision for peace, peoples, and planet Earth.
- Start with personal spiritual transformation, reclaiming the "commission" as a faithful, hopeful caretaker with renewed power and energy.
- Establish small groups to sustain practices of prayer, study, empathy, and action.
- Collect, share, and celebrate stories of progress, improvement, hope, and struggle; share them within communities, congregations, conferences, and regions.
- Strengthen spiritual disciplines privately and within small groups, and attend to the guiding of the Holy Spirit.
- Prayerfully identify the specific responsibilities for action and transformation urgently needed in your region or context (Global South or Global North, urban or rural, powerful or vulnerable, host or sojourner).

Let Us Practice Social and Environmental Holiness

- Organize within our own particular congregations to study and plan what we can do as individuals and members of our churches (for example, congregational "Green Teams" reclaiming the familiar refrain: Think globally, act locally).
- Learn the positions of The United Methodist Church on these issues, and consider the many options for response and action recommended by our General Conference.[50]
- Update our knowledge of; pending legislation, conventions, and treaties concerning nuclear proliferation; and the critical timelines for achieving a truly secure world free of nuclear weapons.
- Connect within our own community groups already active in peace, health, and justice ministries, including energy, immigration, consumerism, discrimination, and population growth.

- Call to accountability public officials and decision makers in local and national governments to eliminate barriers to flourishing and sustainable communities.
- Conserve natural resources and use only renewable resources in every gathering and every ministry of our congregations and our Church.
- Become partners with other groups already active in defending God's creation by teaching others, volunteering in projects, and guiding young people and children in the ways that continue this transformation.
- Interact with those in power over community, national, and international policies to change systems and structures that destroy, deplete, or damage the earth.

Let Us Learn from One Another and Practice Prayerful Self-examination

- Broaden our understanding of these problems and our accountability for them.
- Deepen our relationship with those most affected by the interrelated trio of poverty, environmental degradation, and violence; evaluate our complicity with their causes; and challenge those who ignore their severity.
- Learn how to practice Wesleyan "holy dissatisfaction."
- Take concrete steps as part of God's gracious movement in this broken world.

Let Us Live and Act in Hope

Renewing creation is an act of discipleship for us. It is the work we are called to do, and the One who calls us accompanies us as well, so that we experience a synergy of grace and human responsibility. God is even now "doing a new thing," and we are invited to serve the divine purpose of renewing creation. Despite the threats posed by these interrelated forces, we refuse to be governed by fear. On the stormy waters with his disciples, Jesus admonished them (as he admonishes us) to live in faith rather than fear (Mark 4:35-41). His ministry in the world provides a pattern for us to resist the forces that terrify us without succumbing to them or employing terror. And his resurrection assures us of the new life to come, new life for every element of creation no matter how wounded. The God who raised Jesus from the dead is the God who breathes new life into every aspect of our broken world.

Facing these complex and difficult problems will press us to practice a "responsible hope," one that remains open to promise and peril. "And, given the often overwhelming experiences of life, we must frequently practice hope in pieces, sometimes grieving and shouting, sometimes celebrating. The cumulative effect . . . is a disposition that generates and sustains moral action because it attends to possibilities and limitations. It buoys the spirit and steels the spine."[51]

Included with this document and at the Web site are lists of key resources, other valuable online resources, and key Resolutions from *The United Methodist Book of Resolutions* that are rich in action ideas and educational materials. Also included is a timeline for the studies, action planning in congregations and conferences, and ways to stay connected to share stories of struggle, progress, and hope.

Closing Word of Hope and Blessing

This road is long and the work is hard, so we must see every action we undertake as a *practice of hope*. Through these actions, we put into practice our faith in this divine process of renewing creation. We act in response to God's grace, as followers of Christ Jesus, and in partnership with the Holy Spirit. Our actions then reinforce a disposition of hope that shapes our character as resurrection people, people who believe that death and destruction do not have the last word, people who know that renewal and reconciliation are under way, people who have a passion for the possible. With every action to eradicate poverty and disease, stop the destruction of our natural world, and reverse our reliance on weapons and violence, we put our hope into practice and live out the faith that sustains us.

We close this Foundation Document with a blessing, reminiscent of Wesley's spiritual respiration:

Breathe in the grace and love of God.
Feel the breath renew your spirit and revive your soul.
Breathe out—speaking, acting, and being grace and love in the world.[52]

Notes

1. The United Methodist Council of Bishops, *In Defense of Creation: The Nuclear Crisis and a Just Peace,* "A Pastoral Letter to All United Methodists" (Nashville: Abingdon, 1986).
2. Michael Kinnamon, General Secretary, National Council of Churches, March 10, 2009 at "People of Faith United for Justice" sponsored by the Wisconsin Council of Churches/Interfaith Partners.
3. *In Defense of Creation: The Nuclear Crisis and a Just Peace.*
4. Resolution #367, 2004 *Book of Resolutions* (Resolution #8004, 2008 *BOR*, p. 915).
5. *In Defense of Creation: The Nuclear Crisis and a Just Peace.*
6. In 2002, the Reverend Dr. William Sloane Coffin Jr., referring to a trio of political threats, said, "A more likely and far more dangerous trio would be environmental degradation, pandemic poverty, and a world awash with weapons" (*The Chautauqua Appeal*, with Joan Brown Campbell and Stephen J. Sidorak Jr.).
7. Ibid.
8. Adapted from Bishop Dale White, "Riding Out the Perfect Storm: Communities of Faith Navigate a Scorching Earth," March 2009 for the General Board of Church and Society and Ecumenical Advocacy Days, Washington, D.C.
9. Center for Defense Information. Obtained from: http://www.cdi.org/program/document.cfm?DocumentID=2996
10. Philippines Central Conference, public hearing on *In Defense of Creation* (February 13, 2008).
11. http://www.landmine-action-week.org/statistics.html
12. U.S. Geological Survey, "Report on Consumption of Explosives" at http://www.minerals.usgs.gov/minerals/pubs/commodity/explosives/600401.pdf
13. The late Reverend Sam Dixon, quoted by Melissa Hinnen, "Relief Office in the Philippines Offers Help, Hope," July 28, 2009.
14. Paul Tillich, "The Right to Hope: A Sermon," in *Paul Tillich: Theologian on the Boundaries*, ed. Mark Kline Taylor (Minneapolis: Fortress Press, 1991), 327.
15. "*Works*" refers to *The Works of John Wesley* (Nashville: Abingdon Press Bicentennial Edition, 1984–) unless otherwise noted.
16. Prayer from the Opening Worship of the 40th Year Celebrations, United Theological College of the West Indies.

17. "The Natural World," Social Principles of The United Methodist Church, ¶160.

18. Walter Brueggemann, *Living Toward a Vision: Biblical Reflections on Shalom* (New York: United Church Press, 1982).

19. James Nash, *Loving Nature: Ecological Integrity and Christian Responsibility* (Nashville: Abingdon, 1991), p. 131.

20. http://www.oikoumene.org/en/resources/documents/central-committee/geneva-2008/reports-and-documents/public-issues/minute-on-global-warming-and-climate-change.html

21. "Global Warming and the Poor: A Sheet by the Evangelical Environmental Network," 9/19/08.

22. Liberato Bautista, President of the Conference of Non-Governmental Organizations in Consultative Relationship with the UN, in remarks to the Civil Society Development Forum, July 2, 2009, Geneva.

23. Dwight D. Eisenhower, April 16, 1953, "Chance for Peace," speech before the American Society of Newspaper Editors.

24. Testimony of John Hill, Director Economic and Environmental Justice GBCS to the U.S. House of Representatives Energy and Commerce Subcommittee on "Climate Legislation." www.umc-gbcs.org/site/apps/nlnet/content2.aspx?c=frLJK2PKLqF&b=3631941&ct. Mr. Hill was drawing on the Communiqué of the African College of Bishops, September 2008.

25. *The Chautauqua Appeal to the Religious Communities of America,* 2002 (Endnote 1.).

26. Remarks by President Barack Obama, Hradcany Square, Prague, Czech Republic, April 5, 2009.

27. George Shultz, Henry Kissinger, Sam Nunn, and William Perry roused a resistant political establishment with two op-ed essays in the *Wall Street Journal*, first in January 2007 with follow-up in 2008. See www.nuclearsecurityproject.org for specific goals promoted by the four co-authors.

28. "A Message to the People of The United Methodist Church" from the President of the Council of Bishops, the Chair of the Table of General Secretaries, and the Chair of the Connectional Table, February 2009.

29. Chief Seattle, member of the Duwamish tribe, was a wise, eloquent, and courageous leader of the Suquamish in the Puget Sound area of the U.S. These words are from his famous speech in 1854 to U.S. President Franklin Pierce: "You must teach your children that the ground beneath their feet is the ashes of our grandfathers. So that they will respect the land, tell your children that the earth is rich with the lives of our kin. Teach your children that the earth is our mother, whatever befalls the earth befalls the sons of the earth."

30. See, for example, "Women, Gender Equality, and Climate Change," WomenWatch: Information and Resources on Gender Equality and Empowerment of Women, United Nations: http://www.un.org/womenwatch/feature/climate_change/ Accessed on October 30, 2009.

31. "FAO Strategies for Improving Food Security," UNESCO, at http://www.unesco.org/education/tlsf/TLSF/theme_c/mod14/uncom14t04s01.htm. Accessed October 30, 2009.

32. "Rape in Times of Conflict and War," A Resolution from the General Board of Global Ministries approved by the 1996 General Conference of the United Methodist Church. http://gbgm-umc.org/mission/resolutions/rapewar.html Accessed October 2009.

33. "Women Worldwide Remain Victims of Domestic Violence," March 5, 2008 release of the World Bank on the World Health Organization report, at http://youthink.worldbank.org/4teachers/pdf/gender/story-domesticviolence.pdf Accessed October 30, 2009.

34. World Bank (for statistics from 2005) and United Nations Development Program (for list of items from 1998); obtained from: http://www.globalissues.org/issue/235/consumption-and-consumerism

35. Maude Barlow, "Water as Commodity—The Wrong Prescription," *The Institute for Food and Development Policy, Backgrounder,* Summer 2001, Vol. 7, No. 3. Obtained from: http://www.globalissues.org/article/26/poverty-facts-and-stats#src30

36. "Conventional Arms Transfers to Developing Nations, 2000–2007," U.S. Congressional Research Service. Obtained from: http://www.globalissues.org/article/74/the-arms-trade-is-big-business

37. See, for example, "Statement on Eco-Justice and Ecological Debt," World Council of Churches (February 9, 2009).

38. "In Search of Security," published by the United Methodist Council of Bishops Task Force on Safety and Security, 2004.

39. Social Principles ¶165.A.

40. Twenty-fifth Annual Service of the Caribbean Conference of Churches.

41. Theodore Runyon, *The New Creation: John Wesley's Theology Today* (Nashville: Abingdon Press, 1998), pp. 22-23.

42. Ibid., p. 26.

43. Jürgen Moltmann, *The Spirit of Life: A Universal Affirmation* (Minneapolis: Fortress Press, 1992), pp. 7-8.

44. Resource: Sallie McFague. In accompanying study guides, we may provide additional resources for each of these points. McFague's books (particularly *Super, Natural Christians* [Minneapolis: Fortress, 2003]) are examples of resources for this point in particular.

45. Margaret Farley, *Compassionate Respect: A Feminist Approach to Medical Ethics and Other Questions* (New York: Paulist Press, 2002).

46. Social Principles, "The Social Community," ¶162.

47. Walter Wink, *The Powers That Be: Theology for a New Millennium* (New York: Doubleday, 1999).

48. Social Principles, "The Political Community," ¶164.F.

49. This language comes from the "Initial Statement toward an Ecumenical Declaration on Just Peace," which is part of the World Council of Churches' ecumenical peace convocation planned for 2011.

50. See "Sampling of Related Resolutions of The United Methodist Church" at hopeandaction.org

51. Ellen Ott Marshall, *Though the Fig Tree Does Not Blossom: Toward a Responsible Theology of Christian Hope* (Nashville: Abingdon Press, 2006), p. 107.

52. Ellen Ott Marshall, "Benediction," Claremont School of Theology Chapel, April 30, 2009.

God's Renewed Creation: Call to Hope and Action

Guide for Group Study

To the Leader

In the fall of 2009 the Council of Bishops of The United Methodist Church issued a pastoral letter titled "God's Renewed Creation: Call to Hope and Action." The bishops asked for the Letter to be read aloud in worship, meetings, and other events during and following Advent.

In addition to the Letter, a number of resources including an expanded Foundation Document and a liturgical version of the Letter have been developed to assist congregations as they seek to respond to the bishops' challenges in "God's Renewed Creation." Many of these resources can be found at the Web site www.hopeandaction.org.

The Pastoral Letter and Foundation Document are also available in French, German, Korean, Portuguese, and Spanish at the Web site listed above.

The Council of Bishops is also encouaging all congregations to study the Letter and supporting documents more extensively. This six-session guide has been prepared to assist leaders of groups of adults in congregational and other educational settings as they study and develop plans of action. It is appropriate for study groups at any time of the year.

This study is designed to facilitate conversation and action related to the issues raised in the Pastoral Letter. It challenges participants to look at their congregations and communities, and to take actions that will contribute to a healthier and more peaceful planet.

Each session is designed to last about 90 minutes, and includes reflection upon scripture and prayer as well as study and discussion about the Letter. The hymn "We Utter Our Cry" is used throughout the study with a new stanza being added each week. The words of the hymn are powerful and speak to the themes of the Letter. If your group is not comfortable singing, consider using the hymn as a responsive reading.

In each session participants are asked to read short segments of the Letter and Foundation Document. This provides a common basis for further discussion. The session guide suggests that participants read segments silently. Depending upon the learning preferences of your group, you may want to read the section aloud, or intersperse discussion questions between reading shorter sections.

Throughout the study you will use a simple diagram of the three interconnected threats (pandemic poverty and disease, environmental degradation, and proliferation of weapons and violence). You will be adding information to the diagram each session, so make sure the three interconnected circles are large enough to accommodate these additions.

Another feature of each session is reflection upon one or two of the pledges that the bishops have made in the Letter. As they reflect upon these pledges, the group is encouraged to consider what actions God is calling them to take. As leader you will want to take notes on these discussions so that you can help the group formulate action plans as the study proceeds.

Elements from the liturgical version of the Letter are incorporated into the session worship.

Responsible stewardship of time and resources dictate that this study guide be produced and distributed electronically. Each session includes a one-page leader's guide and a two-page participant piece. We urge you to use the front and back of the paper as you reproduce the participant piece. Some members of your group may wish to skip the paper version completely and read the participant material on laptops or other electronic readers. For those who find it helpful, the guide can be printed out as a booklet on copy machines that have the capacity to print in booklet style.

The Council of Bishops intends for this study to be used not only in local congregations, but also in other settings such as colleges and seminaries. If you are leading the study in a setting beyond the local church, look for ways to help participants make connections to both the context of the group and their local church. For example, in session two you could encourage participants to write letters to the college president as well as to the bishop. In session three you could calculate the carbon footprint of the campus and develop plans to reduce it.

> The Council of Bishops and their task force want to know the results of your study of *God's Renewed Creation: Call to Hope and Action.* Please register your study effort at www.hopeandaction.org ("Contact Us") and encourage the participants to complete the survey at www.surveymonkey.com/s/hopeandaction when the study is completed.

Session One: Leader's Guide

Preparation

• Collect the following materials: newsprint, markers, copies of "Session One: Participant Material," Bibles, *United Methodist Hymnals*. Create a worship center that includes a globe, a Bible, and a candle.

• Post a sheet of newsprint with three overlapping circles labled as in the diagram in the participant material.

• Check out the Web site www.hopeandaction.org for additional stories and information that you may want to incorporate into the session.

1. Introduce the Study

When everyone has arrived, ask people to introduce themselves to the group by telling their names and describing a place in the natural world where they have experienced God's presence.

Point out the items in the worship center and explain that the Bible symbolizes that we are to orient our lives toward God's holy vision; the globe symbolizes the call to practice social and environmental holiness; and the lighted candle symbolizes that we are to live and act in hope.

Explain that during this six-session study the group will be using "God's Renewed Creation: Call to Hope and Action," the Pastoral Letter issued by the United Methodist Council of Bishops as well as the related Foundation Document to explore how they can respond to the three calls illustrated on the worship center.

Read together Romans 8:22-25. Ask the participants to discuss in pairs: Where do you see creation groaning in travail? What is your hope for God's creation that you do not currently see?

2. Read Segments of the Documents

Distribute copies of "Session One: Participant Material" and invite the group to silently read the sections titled "From the Letter" and "From the Foundation Document." Explain that each week they will be reading a segment from the Pastoral Letter and the Foundation Document.

This week's segment introduces three interrelated threats to God's creation. The group will examine these threats in more detail as the study progresses.

Divide the participants into three groups. Assign each group one of the three threats, and ask them to list the words or phrases that come to mind when they hear the assigned threat. These words may include related examples, emotions, results, concerns, and so forth.

Ask one group to read their list aloud. Record their list on the appropriate circle on the newsprint diagram you prepared before class. As they mention an item, discuss whether it applies to either of the other two groups. If so, record it in an overlapping area. (For example, if the proliferation of weapons group listed landmines, that could also relate to poverty, so you would record it in the area where the circles of violence and poverty overlap.)

Continue the process until all groups have reported and recorded their responses. Invite the group to look at the completed diagram and discuss the following questions:

• What surprises you?
• What trends do you see?
• What additional words or phrases would you add to the center of the diagram where all the circles overlap?

3. Reflect on the Pledges

Explain that in the Pastoral Letter, the bishops make a series of pledges. In each session the group will reflect on one or more of these pledges and consider what pledges the participants are willing to make.

Ask the group to read "Pledges." Discuss the following:

• How might we deepen our spiritual consciousness as just stewards of creation?
• What will you do this week to practice hope?

4. Pray Together

Remind the group that in the psalms we find many examples of laments, where people cry out their fears and sorrows to God. Ask the group to read aloud, "We Lament the Wounds on Our Beautiful Planet."

Then invite people to name those wounds on the planet for which they lament. Encourage people to incorporate these laments in their prayer life over the next week.

Sing together the first stanza of "We Utter Our Cry," page 439 in *The United Methodist Hymnal*.

Close with this prayer:

May God's grace purify our reason, strengthen our will, and guide our action. May the love of God, the peace of Christ, and the power of the Holy Spirit be among you, everywhere and always, so that you may be a blessing to all creation and to all the children of God, making peace, nurturing and practicing hope, choosing life and coming to life eternal. Amen.

Encourage the group to explore the items in "Going Further" during the next week.

Session One: Participant Material

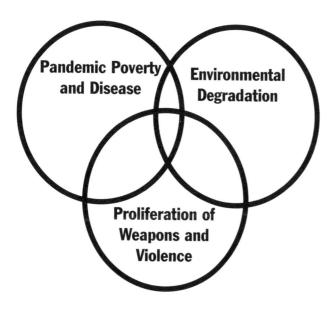

From the Pastoral Letter

God's creation is in crisis. We, the Bishops of The United Methodist Church, cannot remain silent while God's people and God's planet suffer. This beautiful natural world is a loving gift from God, the Creator of all things seen and unseen. God has entrusted its care to all of us, but we have turned our backs on God and on our responsibilities. Our neglect, selfishness, and pride have fostered:

- pandemic poverty and disease,
- environmental degradation, and
- the proliferation of weapons and violence.

Despite these interconnected threats to life and hope, God's creative work continues. Despite the ways we all contribute to these problems, God still invites each one of us to participate in the work of renewal. We must begin the work of renewing creation by being renewed in our own hearts and minds. *We cannot help the world until we change our way of being in it.*

From the Foundation Document

We must prepare our hearts and minds by turning to God and placing all anxiety, loss, and grief before the One who is our ever-present help in time of trouble. And, with God's grace, we remember the story that guides and sustains us, holds us accountable, and gives us hope. It is the story that begins with God's loving gift of creation and culminates in God's promise of renewal for all. It is

the story of the Word made flesh, the Incarnation, God's presence with us. It is the story of Jesus' ministry to the most vulnerable; his denunciation of violence, greed, and oppression; and his call to discipleship. It is the story of resurrection, of the triumph of life over death, and of the promise of new life in Christ. And it is the story of transformation, from old to new, from woundedness to wholeness, and from injustice and violence to the embrace of righteousness and peace.

We have a role to play in this story, but we have not faithfully performed it. God entrusted us with the Creation. But, instead of faithfully caring for our peaceful planet and its people, we have neglected the poor, polluted our air and water, and filled our communities with instruments of war. We have turned our backs on God and one another. By obstructing God's will, we have contributed to pandemic poverty and disease, environmental degradation, and the proliferation of weapons and violence. Around the world, we feel the effects of this interconnected trio in different ways and to varying degrees, but there is no doubt that we all are experiencing elements of the same storm.

The storm builds as powerful forces swirl together:

To affect poverty: the **global economic crisis** as systems built upon self-interest and fraud devastate the global economy; the **resource crisis** as food, water, and energy become scarce; the **justice/poverty** crisis as the gap between rich and poor continues to widen; the **global health crisis** as millions die of the preventable diseases of poverty like malaria, HIV/AIDS, and tuberculosis; and the **refugee crisis** as millions of people are displaced by violence, natural disaster, and loss of jobs.

To affect the environment: the **energy crisis** as oil reserves run out within two or three decades; the **climate crisis** as increasing greenhouse gases threaten to scorch the earth and desertification erodes productive land, polar ice melts, fire seasons lengthen, and coastal floods and severe storms increase in number; the **biodiversity crisis** as at least one-fifth of all plant and animal species face extinction by 2050.

To affect weapons and violence: The **weapons crisis** as the threat of nuclear, biological, and chemical attack looms and precious resources are poured into the sinkhole of futile arms races; the **small arms crisis** as roughly 639 million small arms and light weapons circulate the world and the illegal small arms trade is estimated at close to $1 billion; the **"security" crisis** as global military spending surpasses 1.2 trillion USD in 2007, with the United States spending 45 percent of this amount.

Because these threats are interconnected, each one compounds the effects of the others. This means that people and the planet experience the cumulative effects of this storm. The interrelated nature of these threats also makes it exceedingly difficult to make any real headway on any individual issue. We find ourselves overwhelmed by complex *webs of brokenness*: injustice against migrants, resource scarcity elevated to warfare, energy crises, environmental racism, economic globalization, and violence against the most vulnerable, especially women and girls.

With Open Eyes, We See Relationships

With open eyes, we see the relationships between poverty and disease, environmental degradation, and the proliferation of weapons and violence. Although this makes the problems seem even more difficult to surmount, treating them separately is less effective. To accurately diagnose our situation and craft a viable plan for health, we must see and respond to the ways in which the particular threats interact with one another. For example, we cannot address global poverty without addressing water shortage made worse every day by global warming. We cannot stem the proliferation of weapons without examining dwindling natural resources or minerals as causes of violent conflict. We cannot talk about the need for health care, schools, roads, and wells without reevaluating the amount of money we spend on weapons.

Although we may prioritize poverty and disease, environmental degradation, and weapons differently in light of our individual experiences, we must not lose sight of the connections among them. And we must reject policies and practices that pit the victims of these problems against one another. We must see these problems as linked, like three connected rings, so that a solution for one improves the situation for the others.

Pledges

1. We as your bishops pledge to answer God's call to deepen our spiritual consciousness as just stewards of creation. We commit ourselves to faithful and effective leadership on these issues, in our denomination and in our communities and nations.

8. We pledge to practice hope as we engage and continue supporting the many transforming ministries of our denomination. Every day we will thank God for fruit produced through the work of The United Methodist Church and through each of you.

We Lament the Wounds on Our Beautiful Planet

We see waters polluted, species destroyed, forests ablaze, and land abused. We see weapons and waste littering the earth. We see people, created in the very image of God, suffering from famine and disease, burying their children, and living in hatred and fear. We know the farmers who cannot plant their fields because they are infested by land mines. We know the nations that build and make plans to use weapons of mass destruction in the vain pursuit of security.

Going Further

- The pastoral letter and foundation document can be found at www.hopeandaction.org. Read both documents, particularly looking at the segments covered in this session.

- Pay attention to the number of times you hear issues of pandemic poverty and disease, environmental degradation, and proliferation of weapons and violence mentioned on your local newscast.

- Commit yourself to finding one new example of hope each day.

Session Two: Leader's Guide

Preparation

• Collect the following materials: newsprint, markers, copies of "Session Two: Participant Material," Bibles, *United Methodist Hymnals*, stationery, stamps, worship center from previous session.

• Post a sheet of newsprint with three overlapping circles labeled as you did in the previous session.

• Check out the website www.hopeandaction.org for additional stories and information that you may want to incorporate into the session. Check your annual conference Web site to find the address of your bishop.

1. Introduce the Theme

Begin by inviting people to report examples of pandemic poverty and disease, environmental degradation, and proliferation of weapons and violence that they have heard or read about in the past week. Record the examples in the appropriate circles of the newsprint diagram.

Light the candle as you remind the group of the Pastoral Letter's call: to orient our lives toward God's holy vision, to practice social and environmental holiness, and to live and act in hope. Explain that today's session focuses particularly on practicing social and environmental holiness.

Read aloud Jeremiah 29:4-11. Divide into groups of three and discuss the following questions:

• In thinking about environmental and social holiness, in what ways is your community in "exile"?

• How is your congregation seeking the welfare of the community?

• What images come to your mind when you hear the words, "For surely I know the plans I have for you, says the Lord, plans for your welfare and not for harm, to give you a future with hope"?

Encourage the smaller groups to share with the larger group their insights. Then sing together the first two stanzas of "We Utter Our Cry," page 439 in *The United Methodist Hymnal*.

2. Read Segments of the Documents

Distribute copies of "Session Two: Participant Material" and ask the group to silently read the sections titled "From the Letter" and "From the Foundation Document."

Invite participants to tell stories from their own experiences that illustrate honesty amidst corruption, generosity amidst greed, creation amidst destruction, or passion amidst apathy.

Point out the eight actions listed in the section "Let Us Practice Social and Environmental Holiness," and ask each person to rank the items in order of his or her perception of how well he or she is practicing it. They are to put a one next to the action they feel they are doing the best at, a two in front of the next best, and so forth.

Divide into groups of three and discuss with one another their first and last items. Ask each group to decide on one action they will take during the next week that responds to one of the actions listed. Briefly let each group tell what they intend to do. Explain that during the next session they will have an opportunity to report on what they have done.

3. Reflect on the Pledge

The bishops have pledged that they will advocate for justice and peace in the halls of power in their respective nations and international organizations.

Discuss the following questions:

• Where are the "halls of power" in our community?

• Who are the ones who need an advocate?

• How could we be better advocates for justice and peace as individuals and as a faith community?

Pass out stationery and encourage participants to write a brief note to their bishop letting him or her know of their prayer support as the bishops live out this pledge and the others they have made in the Pastoral Letter.

4. Pray Together

Pray together the lament "We Grieve for Our World, Filled with Pain," printed in the participant material. Ask participants to think of one person they know who is dealing with the issues named in the lament, and to pray silently for that person. Suggest that this week they offer a word of hope and encouragement to that person through a phone call, e-mail, or other communication.

Close by singing again the first two stanzas of "We Utter Our Cry" and praying this prayer:

May God's grace purify our reason, strengthen our will, and guide our action. May the love of God, the peace of Christ, and the power of the Holy Spirit be among you, everywhere and always, so that you may be a blessing to all creation and to all the children of God, making peace, nurturing and practicing hope, choosing life, and coming to life eternal. Amen.

Point out the section titled "Preparing for the Next Session" and assign volunteers to collect the data.

Session Two: Participant Material

From the Pastoral Letter

Second, let us practice social and environmental holiness. We believe personal holiness and social holiness should never be separated. John Wesley preached: "The gospel of Christ knows of no religion, but social. No holiness but social holiness." Through social holiness we make ourselves a channel of God's blessing in the world. Because God's blessing, care, and promise of renewal extend to all of creation, we can speak today of "environmental holiness" as well. We practice social and environmental holiness by caring for God's people and God's planet and by challenging those whose policies and practices neglect the poor, exploit the weak, hasten global warming, and produce more weapons.

From the Foundation Document

It is understandable that looking out on this broken and suffering world would cause despair. But the brokenness and suffering are not the complete story. They are part of our experience, but not the sum total of it. Amidst corruption, there is honesty; amidst greed, there is generosity; amidst killing, there is compassion; amidst destruction, there is creation; amidst devastation, there is preservation; amidst apathy, there is righteous indignation, holy dissatisfaction, and a passion for the possible. If we look carefully, we see seeds of hope that can be cultivated by God's Spirit.

In East Africa, dockworkers refused to off-load a foreign vessel carrying smuggled small arms. Doing what they could to stop the killing in their continent, they also sent word to other dockworkers to refuse the shipment when it arrived farther south.

United Methodists from Lage, Germany forged a partnership with people in Cambine, Mozambique to promote solar energy. They installed solar panels on the local maternity hospital and a theological seminary. The first boy born in the maternity ward after solar light was installed was named "Solarino" to celebrate the renewable energies bringing new life to God's creation.

In a number of U.S. cities, people of faith are working to end the "straw purchase" of handguns—guns that are purchased legally but then passed into the hands of those who could not legally buy them for themselves. Nonviolent volunteers with "Heeding God's Call" raise awareness, they approach gun retailers directly and ask them to accept responsibility for the role they play in violence and to voluntarily end this destructive practice.

Since fourteen people were killed during a workers' strike in 2004 in the Philippines, members of The United Methodist Church and ecumenical groups of adults and young people have organized weekly to visit workers, hear their stories, witness struggles, visit the Congress, circulate petitions, and renew their resolve to work for justice and peace. These life-changing experiences of sharing strengths, fears, and vulnerability, as well as faith and love, empower young people to choose hope amid discouragement.

Stories about our disregard for destruction of one another and the earth more frequently grab the headlines. But acts of perseverance, compassion, care, and positive innovation take place every day in every corner of our world. Right now, there is someone writing a letter to oppose a discriminatory practice or to advocate on behalf of workers treated unjustly, or to support the ratification of a weapons ban. The United Methodist Committee on Relief is setting up disaster response centers and training to "prevent a bad thing from becoming worse." Someone is sitting by a bedside to provide comfort. In a community center, a trainer prepares a group to use methods of nonviolent resistance in order to make a change without violence.

Somewhere, a new school is opening and a new well is functioning. People are unpacking boxes of medical supplies and mosquito nets. Children are educating their parents about global warming, and organizations are examining their carbon footprint. New forms of transportation are coming on the market: hybrid cars and plug-in cars and hydrogen cars and cleaner-burning diesels that do not give children respiratory diseases as they roar through neighborhoods. With the tools of ecumenical organizations, congregations are doing energy audits, recycling materials, replacing energy-guzzling appliances, and installing solar panels and wind turbines.

No matter how discouraging things seem, no matter how overwhelmed and anxious we feel, no matter how apathetic or cynical we become, God is already at work in the world. We must only *open our eyes* to see God's vision, *open our hearts* to receive God's grace, and *open our hands* to do the work God calls us to do.

Let Us Practice Social and Environmental Holiness

Practice personal and social holiness by joining us as we:

- Organize within our own particular congregations to study and plan what we can do as individuals and members of our churches (for example, congregational "Green Teams" reclaiming the familiar refrain: Think Globally, Act Locally)

- Learn the positions of The United Methodist Church on these issues, and consider the many options for response and action recommended by our General Conference

- Update our knowledge of nuclear proliferation; pending legislation, conventions, and treaties, and the critical timelines for achieving a truly secure world free of nuclear weapons

- Connect within our own community groups already active in peace, health, and justice ministries including energy, immigration, consumerism, discrimination, and population growth

- Call to accountability public officials and decision makers in local and national governments to eliminate barriers to flourishing and sustainable communities

And practice environmental holiness with us as we:

- Conserve natural resources and use only renewable resources in every gathering and every ministry of our congregations and Church

- Become partners with other groups already active in defending God's creation by teaching others, volunteering in projects, and guiding young people and children in the ways that continue this transformation

- Interact with those in power over community, national, and international policies to change systems and structures that destroy, deplete, or damage the earth

Pledges

5. *We pledge to advocate for justice and peace in the halls of power in our respective nations and international organizations.*

We Grieve for Our World, Filled with Pain

We see people overwhelmed by fear and anxiety; people who find the wounds of the world too deep to address; people who see the challenges to health and well-being for all as too great to overcome. We know the workers who can no longer provide for their families and the activists exhausted by the struggle for justice.

Preparing for the Next Session

Gather the following information about your congregation. Your pastor, trustees, church maintenance staff, and other church leaders may have helpful information.

Average attendance at weekly services: _____

Number of miles church staff traveled on congregational business in the last year for each transportation mode listed: Auto: _____ Bus: ___ Rail and Subway: _____ Air: _____

Amount of energy the congregation consumed in the past twelve months from each energy source listed:
Electricity:_____ (Kilowatt hours)
Natural Gas:_____ (Million BTUs)
Heating Oil:_____ (Gallons)
Coal: _____(Pounds)

Approximate percent of the congregation's electricity generated by renewable hydropower, wind, solar, or biomass sources. (Local utility office should be able to provide this information.) _____

Number of garbage bags thrown out weekly: _____

Proportion of following waste that is recycled:
Paper: _____ Aluminum: _____ Glass: _____
Plastic: _____ Electronics: _____

Amount of money spent on the following:
Paper and paper products: _____ Office supplies: __
Cleaning supplies and services: _____ Furniture: ____
Construction: _____ Food: _____
Apparel and textiles: _____ Printing: _____
Other goods and services: _____

Going Further

- The Web site www.hopeandaction.org has other articles and stories that relate to the Pastoral Letter.

- Learn about the organizations in your community that advocate for justice and peace. Invite someone from one of those organizations to speak at your church.

- Read "The Natural World" from the Social Principles. (¶160 in *The Book of Discipline of The United Methodist Church*.)

Session Three: Leader's Guide

Preparation

• Collect the following materials: newsprint diagram from previous session, markers, copies of "Session Three: Participant Material," Bibles, *United Methodist Hymnals*, worship center from previous sessions.

• If possible, arrange for a computer with Internet access and a projector. If not, follow the directions in "Reflect on the Pledge" to calculate the congregational carbon footprint, and print out the results before the session.

• Check out the Web site www.hopeandaction.org for additional stories and information that you may want to incorporate into the session.

1. Introduce the Theme

Remind the participants that during the last session, participants planned to take an action related to practicing social and environmental holiness. Encourage participants to report what they did and learned. Using a different color of marker, note the actions in the appropriate circle on the newsprint diagram from last week. (For example, learning about pending treaties related to nuclear proliferation might be noted in the overlapping of the proliferation of weapons circle and environmental degradation circle.)

Recall the symbolism of the Bible, the globe, and the candle on the worship center: to orient our lives toward God's holy vision, to practice social and environmental holiness, and to live and act in hope.

Ask a volunteer to read Matthew 5:14-16 as you light the candle. In small groups discuss the following:

• In relationship to the three symbols on the worship center, where have you experienced God's light shining through others? God's light shining through you?

• What resources and gifts are we hiding under bushel baskets instead of utilizing them for the glory of God and to the benefit of God's good earth?

Encourage the smaller groups to share their insights with the larger group. Then sing together the first three stanzas of "We Utter Our Cry," page 439 in *The United Methodist Hymnal*.

2. Read Segments of the Documents

Distribute copies of "Session Three: Participant Material" and ask the group to silently read the sections titled "From the Letter" and "From the Foundation Document."

To help the group get a sense of the inequity in the amount of resources consumed and waste produced, count the number of people in the group and ask for volunteers to multiply that number by the following numbers: (a) 11, (b) 20, (c) 25, (d) 27, (e) 44, (f) 100. As the numbers are reported, explain that it represents the number of people in the indicated country that use about the same amount of particular resources as the class.

a) Paper use in Romania.
b) Carbon dioxide emissions in the Philippines.
c) Meat consumption in Malawi.
d) Total energy consumption in the Democratic Republic of the Congo.
e) Motor vehicle gasoline in Peru.
f) Electricity use in Nigeria.

Discuss the following questions:
• How do you feel when you hear these numbers?
• What are potentially negative and positive ways of responding to these feelings?

3. Reflect on the Pledge

The bishops have pledged to measure the carbon footprint of our episcopal and denominational offices, determine how to reduce it, and implement those changes. They are challenging congregations to do the same.

Go to www.coolcongregations.com/calculator/ and use the information that people were previously assigned to gather (Session Two: "Preparing for the Next Session") to calculate the congregational carbon footprint.

Discuss the steps needed to develop and implement a plan to reduce the congregational footprint. Make assignments for taking the first step.

4. Pray Together

Pray together the lament, "We Weep for Communities in Crisis," printed in the participant material, followed by a time of silent prayer. Close by singing again the first three stanzas of "We Utter Our Cry" and praying this prayer:

May God's grace purify our reason, strengthen our will, and guide our action. May the love of God, the peace of Christ, and the power of the Holy Spirit be among you, everywhere and always, so that you may be a blessing to all creation and to all the children of God, making peace, nurturing and practicing hope, choosing life, and coming to life eternal. Amen.

Encourage the group to explore the items in "Going Further" during the next week.

Session Three: Participant Material

From the Pastoral Letter

We all feel saddened by the state of the world, overwhelmed by the scope of these problems, and anxious about the future, but *God calls us and equips us to respond.* No matter how bad things are, God's creative work continues. Christ's resurrection assures us that death and destruction do not have the last word. Paul taught that through Jesus Christ, God offers redemption to all of creation and reconciles all things, "whether on earth or in heaven" (Colossians 1:20). God's Spirit is always and everywhere at work in the world fighting poverty, restoring health, renewing creation, and reconciling peoples.

From the Foundation Document

With Open Hearts, We Acknowledge Our Complicity

In our discussion "The World Community" in the Social Principles of The United Methodist Church, we acknowledge this fact: "Some nations possess more military and economic power than do others" (¶165.B). Some nations consume more of the world's resources, generate more of the world's waste, and produce more of the world's weapons. For example:

- Twenty percent of the world's population accounts for 76% of private consumption of things like electricity, paper, meat and fish, and vehicle usage.
- "A mere 12% of the world's population uses 85% of its water, and these 12% do not live in the Third World."
- The United States is the largest supplier of conventional weapons in the world, selling 38% of all weapons purchased between 2000 and 2007—roughly one-half of these weapons were sold or transferred to developing countries.

There are many ways to designate the differences between us: Global North and Global South; first world and third world; first world and two-thirds world; developed world and developing world. We must also acknowledge that there is deep poverty and underdevelopment in the so-called first world, and there are pockets of wealth and opulence in the so-called third world.

Our social and economic situations are much more complex than any labels or statistics can capture. And yet, some generalizations are also true and important. Those of us in the Global North consume more, waste more, and militarize more than those of us in the second category. We in the North must take responsibility for the environmental damage we have caused, what many now call our "environmental or ecological debt." We must reckon with our vain pursuit of security through weapons and violence. We must also confess the greed and selfishness that motivate us to pursue our own comfort while ignoring those in need.

We also recognize that "no nation or culture is absolutely just and right in its treatment of its own people." We in the Global South must acknowledge corruption that threatens our societies. Like our brothers and sisters in the north, we too must challenge our nations' quest for security through weaponry. When we spend precious resources on weapons, we are stealing from the poor of our country. We confess selfishness and greed, made worse in contexts of scarcity.

We join together in acknowledging that we have resources and gifts that we hide under bushel baskets (Matthew 5:15) instead of utilizing them for the glory of God and to the benefit of God's good earth. We have opportunities for charity and justice making that we do not exercise. We have also failed to encourage the gifts and energies of our young people by not involving them in community building, leadership, and development. And we have not done enough to stop violence against women and children. At times we all fall prey to despair, losing sight of God's presence with us and failing to hear God's call to us. We ask for God's help and grace as we turn away from harmful practices and commit ourselves to God's purpose of renewal for all.

Pledge

6. We pledge to measure the "carbon footprint" of our episcopal and denominational offices, determine how to reduce it, and implement those changes. We will urge our congregations, schools, and ministries to do the same.

We Weep for Communities in Crisis

We see communities without basic health care and clean water; communities stripped of natural resources and denied access to land; communities torn apart by intolerance, religious extremism, and ethnic hatred. We know the refugee who risks death and capture searching for a safe place to live.

Going Further

- The Web site www.hopeandaction.org has other articles and stories that relate to the Pastoral Letter.

- Read "The World Community" from the Social Principles (¶165 in *The Book of Discipline of The United Methodist Church*).

- To learn more about how your resource usage compares to those in other areas of the world, go to www.earthtrends.wri.org

- Go to http://coolclimate.berkeley.edu and use the carbon footprint calculator to calculate your household's carbon footprint. Note how your footprint compares to the world average. Develop a plan to reduce your footprint by four metric tons.The following suggestions will help you get started:

- Use energy-saving compact fluorescent lightbulbs instead of incandescent lightbulbs.

- Stop using plastic grocery bags. Take reusable canvas bags with you to the grocery store. Your congregation may even want to consider providing reusable bags with the church name as a welcome for newcomers.

- Don't wash partial loads of dishes or clothes; wait until you have a full load.

- Incorporate a few meatless days into your regular meal planning.

- Turn the temperature of your house down one degree when the furnace is running and up one degree when the air conditioner is running.

- Only plug in your phone charger and other charging units when you are actually charging.

- Eat local produce.

- Plant a church garden.

Session Four: Leader's Guide

Preparation

• Collect the following materials: newsprint diagram from previous sessions, markers, copies of "Session Four: Participant Material," Bibles, *United Methodist Hymnals*, worship center from previous sessions.

• Check out the Web site www.hopeandaction.org for additional stories and information that you may want to incorporate into the session.

1. Introduce the Theme

Review the steps you developed in the previous session to reduce the congregational carbon footprint. Report any progress that has been made, and continue with any planning that needs to occur.

Light the candle as you recall the symbolism of the Bible, the globe, and the candle on the worship center: to orient our lives toward God's holy vision, to practice social and environmental holiness, and to live and act in hope.

Divide into three groups and assign each group one of the three interrelated threats. Ask participants to focus on the assigned threat as they listen to Matthew 19:23-26.

Then break into groups of three, so that each group has one person who was focusing on each threat. Ask them to discuss the following questions:

• How do you think this scripture relates to the threat you focused on?

• What word of hope do you find in the scripture?

Encourage participants to record their words of hope in the appropriate circles on the newsprint diagram.

Then sing together the first four stanzas of "We Utter Our Cry," page 439 in *The United Methodist Hymnal*.

2. Read Segments of the Documents

Distribute copies of "Session Four: Participant Material" and ask the group to silently read the sections titled "From the Letter." and "From the Foundation Document."

Use the following questions as a springboard for further discussion:

• Where do these segments of the Letter and Foundation Document intersect with your passions?

• What do you want to learn more about?

Dividing back into the three previous groups, ask each to identify existing organizations (local, national, world) that are working to develop solutions to the assigned threat. As each group reports back, write the names of the organizations in the appropriate circle of the newsprint diagram. Ask who from the congregation is involved with any of the organizations listed. Place a star next to those.

Consider asking those named to write an article for the church newsletter, create a bulletin board, speak to a church gathering, or develop some other way to inform the congregation about the work of the organization.

3. Reflect on the Pledges

Ask participants to read "Pledges" in the participant material. Ask them to recall their earliest memory of being in conversation with someone whose life experience was dramatically different from their own. Encourage participants to tell these memories, reflecting on the following questions:

• What did I learn from the experience?

• In what ways was my life enriched?

• Were there any long-term results of the conversation?

Then ask them to recall their most recent memory of being in conversation with someone whose life experience was dramatically different. Encourage participants to tell their stories, reflecting on the previous questions.

Brainstorm a list of opportunities for participants to engage in dialogue with people who have different life experience. These could be as simple as visiting a restaurant frequented by immigrants and engaging in conversation with the workers, to more formal things such as enrolling in an interfaith dialogue experience. Encourage each person to select one thing that they will do in the next week.

4. Pray Together

Pray together the lament, "We Mourn a World of Inequality and Injustice," printed in the participant material followed by a time of silent prayer. Close by singing again the first four stanzas of "We Utter Our Cry" and praying this prayer:

May God's grace purify our reason, strengthen our will, and guide our action. May the love of God, the peace of Christ, and the power of the Holy Spirit be among you, everywhere and always, so that you may be a blessing to all creation and to all the children of God, making peace, nurturing and practicing hope, choosing life, and coming to life eternal. Amen.

Encourage the group to explore the items in "Going Further" during the next week.

Session Four: Participant Material

From the Pastoral Letter

God is already visibly at work in people and groups around the world. We rededicate ourselves to join these movements, the movements of the Spirit. Young people are passionately raising funds to provide mosquito nets for their "siblings" thousands of miles away. Dockworkers are refusing to off-load small weapons being smuggled to armed combatants in civil wars in their continent. People of faith are demanding land reform on behalf of landless farm workers. Children and young people have formed church-wide "green teams" to transform our buildings and ministries into testimonies of stewardship and sustainability. Ecumenical and interreligious partners persist in demanding the major nuclear powers to reduce their arsenals, step by verifiable step, making a way to a more secure world totally disarmed of nuclear weapons. God is already doing a new thing. With this Letter and the accompanying Foundation Document, we rededicate ourselves to participate in God's work, and we urge you all to rededicate yourselves as well.

From the Foundation Document

Call to Hope and Action

John Wesley insisted, "The gospel of Christ knows of no religion, but social. No holiness but social holiness. Faith working by love is the length and breadth and depth and height of Christian perfection." (*Preface to Hymns and Sacred Poems*, 1739, ¶ 5) Ours is not solely a private faith, but one that also orients us toward God *and* the needs of our neighbor and world. At a time when people are cynical about religion, United Methodists must continue our rich heritage of "faith working by love" as an example of the church's ability to make a positive difference in the world.

The leaders and members of our denomination have a long tradition of speaking truth to power, naming injustice and advocating for right relationships and equitable sharing among all God's peoples. Today, United Methodists protest racism and abuse directed toward illegal immigrants and challenge local and federal authorities to maintain a democracy open to all people. In Arizona, Bishop Minerva Carcaño joins thousands in protest, and in Texas, United Methodist Women and the Board of Church and Society organize interreligious prayer vigils that include people from ten different countries.

We feel the energy in thousands of ministries every day in our United Methodist connection. We are strengthened and inspired by the Toberman Neighborhood House in San Pedro, California, which provides services for gang prevention and gang intervention, family counseling and mental health, child care, and community organizing. The Toberman House is one of 100 national mission institutions, founded by the women of the Methodist tradition in 1903 and still supported by UMW Mission Giving.

Today, we are increasingly aware of the powerful role that young adults are playing to transform our societies and to challenge our church to live out its commitments to social justice, creation care, and peace. For example, every year, young adult interns with the Micah Corps in the Nebraska Annual Conference immerse themselves in social justice education, training, and advocacy on behalf of the poor and marginalized in their state.

During the many listening and learning events that informed the Pastoral Letter and Foundation Document, participants did much more than articulate their concern about poverty and disease, environmental degradation, and weapons and violence. From ages ten to one hundred, they expressed their deep desire to do something about these problems and their great hope that change is possible. These conversations raised awareness about several things:

1. We must study, observe, learn from, and listen to one another, especially to victims of these threats. Some of us are indeed aware of these problems, but less aware of the interconnections, and even less aware of our personal connections and complicity or the dramatic urgency in what is already happening in our communities. We must listen with particular care to our young people, whose knowledge, consciousness, and impatience for action can be energizing and inspiring for us all.

2. We can be re-energized and spiritually renewed by the examples from our own Wesleyan and United Methodist heritage and experience. We belong to an amazing denomination with transforming potential already active and agile in thousands of ministry settings including legislatures, parliaments, and congresses.

3. We need an ongoing word of hope as we follow Wesley out into the streets and communities to face uncomfortable and difficult things and connect with others working for justice, peace, and the integrity of creation.

4. "With God all things are possible" (Matthew 19:26). We have immense hope, and it will grow as we study, act, and connect.

Pledges

3. We pledge to practice dialogue with those whose life experience differs dramatically from our own, and we pledge to practice prayerful self-examination. For example, in the Council of Bishops, the fifty active bishops in the United States are committed to listening and learning with the nineteen active bishops in Africa, Europe, Asia, and the Philippines. And the bishops representing the conferences in the United States will prayerfully examine the fact that their nation consumes more than its fair share of the world's resources, generates the most waste, and produces the most weapons.

4. We pledge ourselves to make common cause with religious leaders and people of goodwill worldwide who share these concerns. We will connect and collaborate with ecumenical and interreligious partners and with community and faith organizations so that we may strengthen our common efforts.

We Mourn a World of Inequality and Injustice

We see a world where some live opulently while others barely survive; a world where the innocent suffer and the corrupt profit; a world where too many still find their opportunities and freedom limited by skin color, gender, or birthplace. We know the boy who is caught in the snare of drugs and violence and the girl who is raped or forced into prostitution.

Going Further

- The Web site www.hopeandaction.org has other articles and stories that relate to the Pastoral Letter.
- Read more about the Toberman Neighborhood Center at www.toberman.org
- Read about the experiences of the Micah Corps at http://micah-corps.blogspot.com
- Read John Wesley's sermon "The Character of a Methodist." It can be found at http://new.gbgm-umc.org/umhistory/wesley

---

Session Five: Leader's Guide

Preparation

• Collect the following materials: newsprint diagram from previous sessions, pencils, copies of "Session Five: Participant Material," Bibles, *United Methodist Hymnals*, and worship center from previous sessions.

• Check out the Web site www.hopeandaction.org for additional stories and information that you may want to incorporate into the session.

1. Introduce the Theme

Encourage people to report any experiences they have had since the previous session of engaging in dialogue with those whose life experience is dramatically different from their own.

Light the candle as you recall the symbolism of the Bible, the globe, and the candle on the worship center: to orient our lives toward God's holy vision, to practice social and environmental holiness, and to live and act in hope.

Explain that this session particularly emphasizes living and acting in hope. Ask the participants to focus on the lighted candle as they listen to you read Isaiah 43:18-21 twice, pausing between readings for silent reflection.

Then in small groups ask them to discuss the following questions:

• What images emerged as you listened to the scripture?
• Where have you experienced God doing a "new thing" in your own life?
• What "new thing" do you think God is about to do in your congregation?
• What word of hope did you hear?

Then sing together the first five stanzas of "We Utter Our Cry," page 439 in *The United Methodist Hymnal*.

2. Read Segments of the Documents

Distribute copies of "Session Five: Participant Material" and ask the group to silently read the sections titled "From the Letter" and "From the Foundation Document." As they read, ask them to underline what they believe are the five most important words or phrases.

Then have them report what they have underlined, recording the words or phrases on newsprint. When all the responses have been recorded, look for common themes that have emerged. Encourage honest discussion about why people selected what they did.

Divide into small groups and challenge each group to select one sentence either from the Pastoral Letter or the Foundation Document that speaks most forcefully of hope in relationship to the three interrelated threats, or to write a sentence of their own.

As the groups report, record the sentences around the edges of the newsprint diagram you have used in previous sessions, so that the three interrelated threat circles are surrounded by the statements of hope.

3. Reflect on the Pledges

Ask participants to read "Pledges" in the participant material. Discuss the following questions:

• What would make our community a "greener" place?
• What resources (people, facilities, money, information, and so forth) could our congregation contribute to the effort?
• Where do we need assistance? From whom?
• How can we share what we have learned with our congregation and our community?

4. Pray Together

Lead the group in the confession in the participant material. After the unison part of the confession, encourage the participants to name aloud or silently personal confessions related to being the stewards and caretakers that God created us to be. Sing together stanza five of "We Utter Our Cry" as a response to the confession. Close with the following prayer:

May God's grace purify our reason, strengthen our will, and guide our action. May the love of God, the peace of Christ, and the power of the Holy Spirit be among you, everywhere and always, so that you may be a blessing to all creation and to all the children of God, making peace, nurturing and practicing hope, choosing life, and coming to life eternal. Amen.

Encourage the group to explore the items in "Going Further" during the next week, particularly rereading the entire Pastoral Letter and Foundation Document.

Session Five: Participant Material

From the Pastoral Letter

Third, let us live and act in hope. As people in the tradition of John Wesley, we understand reconciliation and renewal to be part of the *process* of salvation that is already underway. We are not hemmed into a fallen world. Rather we are part of a divine unfolding process to which we must contribute. As we faithfully respond to God's grace and call to action, the Holy Spirit guides us in this renewal. With a resurrection spirit, we look forward to the renewal of the whole creation and commit ourselves to that vision. We pray that God will accept and use our lives and resources that we rededicate to a ministry of peace, justice, and hope to overcome poverty and disease, environmental degradation, and the proliferation of weapons and violence.

From the Foundation Document

For many hundreds of years "The People of the Book"—Jews, Christians, and Muslims—have lived through hard times of drought, fire, floods, raging waters, and tempestuous winds, sustained by the ancient wisdom of the psalmists, who over and over again sang of "the steadfast love of the Lord."

Today, the human family is awakening to alarming news: after several thousand years of a stable climate that enabled us to thrive, the earth is heating up at an accelerating rate. Climate change poses a particular threat to the world's poor because it increases the spread of diseases like malaria and causes conflicts over dwindling natural resources. Easy access to small arms ensures that such conflicts turn deadly, and the specter of a nuclear war that would destroy the earth continues to loom over us.

Clearly we have arrived at "a hinge of history," a revolutionary time of great challenge. We turn again to the ancient wisdom and remember the ringing challenge of God: "Behold, I am doing a new thing; now it springs forth, do you not perceive it?" (Isaiah 43:19). Do we not see signs that God is at work in this crisis?

As the earth is being transformed, God has blessed human beings with the capacity to read the signs of the times and to respond with intelligence and faith.

Learned scientists and experts monitor the changes that have an impact our very survival. They are clarifying the measures we must take immediately to save our forests, oceans, air, and human and animal ecosystems.

More than that, God has inspired human beings to envision new futures and to invent the tools necessary to make them a reality: technologies to replace fossil fuels with energy from the wind and sun; new forms of transportation, "green jobs," and guides for reducing "carbon footprints." Thousands and thousands of persons in faith-based and community-based coalitions, congregations, businesses, and farms are already acting for change in quiet, persistent, and profound ways.

Even further, God is bringing people together to plan and to act upon emerging realities. Villages, towns, and local governments urge and guide neighbors to share common cause; cities, states, and nations identify the special needs of their citizens and implement solutions; the United Nations and international agencies research global problems, identify solutions, and shape the organizations to address them. Public leaders are working at a feverish pace to reshape the rules of engagement between humans and the earth. Empowering all these efforts is an amazing network of globe-circling monetary, industrial, transportation, and communications systems such as the human family has never before known.

Finally, Christian and interreligious communities are speaking out boldly on the interrelated nature of the present crisis. For example, the "Ecumenical Declaration on Just Peace" currently being drafted by the World Council of Churches names justice, peace, and the integrity of creation.

Why is all of this activity happening? Because the peoples of the world are reading the signs carefully—we see clearly that God is doing a new thing, and that God is inviting the human family to participate in transformation. . . .

We open our hearts to confess our sin, to receive God's grace, to discern God's call, and to feel strengthened by God's sustaining Spirit. We are not initiating these actions; rather we are responding to God's gracious invitation to join God's renewal of creation. God invites us, with all of our imperfections, to participate in this work. We open our hearts so that we can change. We open our hearts to feel God's presence with us as we labor. We open our hearts "that we may anchor our souls in the One who is just, who renews our strength for the work to be done."

We open our hearts to embody the "moral image of God," to use Wesley's words (*Works* 2:188). This moral image is not something we possess but is ours only insofar as we continually receive it from the Source. We embody the moral image of God as we receive God's grace and then reflect that grace out into the world. To describe this process of receiving and reflecting God's grace Wesley used the image of breath, calling it "spiritual respiration": "God's breathing into the soul, and the soul's breathing back what it first receives from God; a continual *action* of God upon the soul, the *re-action* of the soul upon God" (*Works* 1:442).

We open our hands to respond to the Spirit and do the work God calls us to do in the world. As human beings created in God's image, we have a special responsibility to care for the gift of creation. Wesley calls this "the political image of God" (*Works* 2:188). We often live as though "being created in God's image" gives us special privilege, but living with that assumption is a grave mistake. Our status as human beings increases our *responsibility*, not our *privilege*. Being created in God's image means that we are charged with caring for this world, not invited to abuse it. Doing justice, building peace, and mending the planet are ways that we take care of what we have been given. However, we are not caretakers for an absentee landlord; rather God's renewing Spirit works through us and courses around us breathing new life into the planet and its people. . . .

Renewing creation is an act of discipleship for us. It is the work we are called to do, and the One who calls us accompanies us as well, so that we experience a synergy of grace and human responsibility. God is even now "doing a new thing," and we are invited to serve the divine purpose of renewing creation. Despite the threats posed by these interrelated forces, we refuse to be governed by fear. On the stormy waters with his disciples, Jesus admonished them (and admonishes us) to live in faith rather than fear (Mark 4:35-41). His ministry in the world provides a pattern for us to resist the forces that terrify us without succumbing to them or employing terror. And his resurrection assures us of the new life to come, new life for every element of creation no matter how wounded. The God who raised Jesus from the dead is the God who breathes new life into every aspect of our broken world.

Facing these complex and difficult problems will press us to practice a "responsible hope," one that remains open to promise and peril. "And, given the often overwhelming experiences of life, we must frequently practice hope in pieces, sometimes grieving and shouting, sometimes celebrating. The cumulative effect . . . is a disposition that generates and sustains moral action because it attends to possibilities and limitations. It buoys the spirit and steels the spine."

Pledges

7. *We pledge to provide, to the best of our ability, the resources needed by our conferences to dramatically reduce our collective exploitation of the planet, peoples, and communities, including technical assistance with buildings and programs, education and training, and young people's and online networking resources.*

9. *We pledge more effective use of the church and community Web pages to inspire and to share what we learn.* We celebrate the communications efforts that tell the stories of struggle and transformation within our denomination.

Confession

Leader: God sees the creation's wounds. God hears our lament. And God calls us to accountability. We cannot be instruments of God's renewal if we deny our complicity in pandemic poverty and disease, environmental degradation, and proliferation of weapons and violence.

All: As United Methodists, we confess our failure to embody the image of God. We rationalize our sin; satisfy our own desires; and exercise our freedom at the expense of the common good. We know that we should live within sustainable boundaries but we struggle to summon the moral will to change. As individuals and communities of faith, we have not been the stewards and caretakers that God created us to be.

Going Further

- The Web site www.hopeandaction.org has other articles and stories that relate to the Pastoral Letter.

- Reread the entire Pastoral Letter and Foundation Document found at www.hopeandaction.org. Reflect on what you have learned in the study of the documents.

Session Six: Leader's Guide

Preparation

• Collect the following materials: newsprint diagram from previous sessions, pencils, copies of "Session Six: Participant Material," Bibles, *United Methodist Hymnals*, worship center from previous sessions.

• Check out the Web site www.hopeandaction.org for additional stories and information that you may want to incorporate into the session.

1. Introduce the Theme

Light the candle as you recall the symbolism of the Bible, the globe, and the candle on the worship center: to orient our lives toward God's holy vision, to practice social and environmental holiness, and to live and act in hope.

Explain that this session particularly focuses on orienting our lives towards God's holy vision.

Divide the participants into three groups. As they listen to you read Luke 10:25-28, ask one group to imagine they are the lawyer, another group to imagine they are Jesus, and the third group to imagine they are a bystander watching the exchange.

After you have read the scripture, ask them to divide into groups of three, so that each triad has a member from each of the original three groups.

In the triads have them discuss the following questions:

• What did you see, smell, hear, and feel?
• What do you think the lawyer probably did afterward?
• What does this scripture say to us today related to orienting our lives to God's holy vision?

Then sing together all six stanzas of "We Utter Our Cry," page 439 in *The United Methodist Hymnal*.

2. Read Segments of the Documents

Distribute copies of "Session Six: Participant Material" and ask the group to silently read the sections titled "From the Letter" and "From the Foundation Document." Discuss the following questions:

• Looking at the world through eyes of faith, where do you see love at work? Where is transformation happening in your community?
• The Foundation Document names several ways in which we love God and neighbors; are some more important than others? If so, which ones?

Brainstorm ways the congregation can live out the items listed in the section "Let Us Order Our Lives Toward God's Holy Vision."

3. Reflect on the Pledge

Ask participants to read "Pledge" in the participant material. Together make a list of decisions that have been made by groups in the church recently. This could include the Church Council, church committees, United Methodist Women and Men, the youth group, trustees, and so forth. Review each decision and discuss what decision might have been made if each group had asked: Does this contribute to God's renewal of creation? Or if the question was asked, how did it affect the decision? Consider ways the question could become a regular part of the church planning process.

Then ask participants to think about personal decisions they are facing and how asking the question might influence those decisions.

4. Evaluate the Study

Give each person a sheet of paper and ask them to finish the following sentences.

• One thing I have learned during this study is . . .
• I have changed my thinking about . . .
• I have started . . .
• I have stopped . . .
• In six months I hope our church . . .
• In ten years I hope our world . . .

Allow those who wish to share their answers.

Encourage people when they go home to respond to the survey listed in "Going Further."

• As a group discuss the following questions:
• What have we learned?
• What actions have we taken?
• What actions do we plan to take?
• What will we be praying about?

5. Pray Together

Lead "Rededication" from the Participant Material. Sing "We Utter Our Cry" as a response. Close with the following prayer:

May God's grace purify our reason, strengthen our will, and guide our action. May the love of God, the peace of Christ, and the power of the Holy Spirit be among you, everywhere and always, so that you may be a blessing to all creation and to all the children of God, making peace, nurturing and practicing hope, choosing life, and coming to life eternal. Amen.

Session Six: Participant Material

From the Pastoral Letter

Aware of God's vision for creation, we no longer see a list of isolated problems affecting disconnected people, plants, and animals. Rather, we see one interconnected system that is "groaning in labor pains" (Romans 8:22). The threats to peace, people, and planet earth are related to one another, and God's vision encompasses complete well-being. We, your bishops, join with many global religious leaders to call for a comprehensive response to these interrelated issues. We urge all United Methodists and people of goodwill to offer themselves as instruments of God's renewing Spirit in the world.

First, let us orient our lives toward God's holy vision. This vision of the future calls us to hope and to action. "For surely I know the plans I have for you, says the LORD, plans for your welfare and not for harm, to give you a future with hope" (Jeremiah 29:11). Christ's resurrection assures us that this vision is indeed a *promise* of renewal and reconciliation. As disciples of Christ, we take God's promise as the purpose for our lives. Let us, then, rededicate ourselves to God's holy vision, living each day with awareness of the future God extends to us and of the Spirit that leads us onward.

From the Foundation Document

When we open our eyes to God's vision of renewal, we also clearly see the ways in which we obstruct God's process. When we open our eyes to the presence of God's renewing Spirit in the world, we celebrate every charitable act, every just practice, every courageous stand for peace, every moment of reconciliation, every cessation of violence, and every restored habitat as a glimpse of the Kingdom of God, as a "seed-like presence of that which is hoped for."

We might think of opening our eyes as a spiritual discipline rooted in John Wesley's understanding of the "natural image of God" (*Works* 2:188). Three gifts are included in the basic equipment our Creator has given us as spiritual beings to be both independent and at the same time to relate to God and our neighbor. The first of these gifts is *reason*—the human ability to discern order and relationships, to grasp how things work, and to make judgments. The second gift is our *will*—the ability to commit ourselves to God, to persons, and to goals, and to carry through. The third gift is our *freedom*. God does not want automatons. "A mere machine" is not morally answerable, says Wesley. Human responsibility requires freedom (*Works* [Jackson] 10:234).

Therefore, we reflect the natural image of God when we exercise our reason for accurate understanding and good judgment, and when we respond to God's grace by freely exercising our will to choose good and resist evil. We open our eyes in order to perceive the world accurately, understand our roles and responsibilities, and exercise good judgment. . . .

In order to live fully in God's image, we must make God's promise our purpose. We respond to the groaning of creation *and* to this vision of renewal by making ourselves a channel of God's blessing. We open our hearts to receive God's grace, and we open our hands in response, to do the work God calls us to do. What does it really mean to fashion ourselves as instruments of God's renewing Spirit? This is not a new question. It is, in fact, a variation of the question posed to Jesus many times. "What must I do to inherit eternal life?" (Luke 10:25). Jesus answers with the dual love commandment: "You shall love the Lord your God with all your heart, and with all your soul, and with all your mind. This is the great and first commandment. And a second is like it, You shall love your neighbor as yourself" (Matthew 22:37-39). Participating in God's work of renewal looks like love shining forth in action.

We love God by paying attention to God's creation. We pay attention to poverty, environmental degradation, and weapons and violence. Neglecting these ills and those who suffer their effects is contrary to love. We respond to Jesus' commandment by paying attention to our world. And we begin to fashion ourselves as instruments of God's renewal by deepening our spiritual consciousness as faithful stewards and directing our attention to the world God loves.

We love God and neighbor by practicing compassionate respect. We extend our care and concern, and provide assistance and comfort as needed. But we also respect the ones cared for as subjects in their own right. We respect the earth, knowing that it is not ours to plunder. We respect those suffering poverty and disease, granting them full autonomy to determine their own needs and path to well-being. We respect victims of violence by supporting their pursuit of a just peace. In sum, we "work toward societies in which each person's value is recognized, maintained, and strengthened."

We love God and neighbor by changing our behavior. We cannot be instruments of love if we hold on to selfishness and greed. Jesus calls us to love, but he also calls us to conversion, to a radical change in our lifestyle and attitude. His message is clear: We cannot help the world until we change our own way of being in it.

We love God and neighbor by challenging those who do harm. We must not only respond to the suffering already created, but also challenge people, companies, and governments that continue to exploit the weak, destroy the earth, perpetuate violence, and generate more weapons. We follow Jesus' example of confronting authorities nonviolently, using the force of love. And we adhere to our Social Principles, which affirm the "right of individuals to dissent when acting under the constraint of conscience."

Anyone who has experienced genuine love knows its power. Looking at the world through the eyes of faith, we can see love at work, transforming an abandoned lot into a community garden, transforming a neglected child into a healthy and happy toddler, and transforming people at war into communities committed to reconciliation. We witness God's work of renewal in these pockets of transformation. And we participate in that work of renewal by living fully as Christ's disciples, people whose love of God and neighbor shines forth in action.

Let Us Order Our Lives Toward God's Holy Vision

- Renew our understandings of God's holy vision for peace, peoples, and planet Earth.
- Start with personal spiritual transformation reclaiming the "commission" as a faithful, hopeful caretaker with renewed power and energy;
- Establish small groups to sustain practices of prayer, study, empathy, and action;
- Collect, celebrate and share stories of progress, improvement, hope and struggle; share them within communities, congregations, conferences, and regions;
- Strengthen spiritual disciplines privately and within small groups, and attend to the guiding of the Holy Spirit;
- Prayerfully identify the specific responsibilities for action and transformation urgently needed in your region or context (Global South or Global North, urban or rural, powerful or vulnerable, host or sojourner).

Pledge

2. *We pledge to make God's vision of renewal our goal.* With every evaluation and decision, we will ask: Does this contribute to God's renewal of creation? Ever aware of the difference between what is and what must be, we pledge to practice Wesleyan "holy dissatisfaction."

Rededication

Leader: Find solace and strength in the knowledge that God's creative work continues. This gracious and loving God still calls us forth and prepares us to care for one another and the planet. With John Wesley, let us all affirm the "unceasing presence of God, the loving, pardoning God, manifested to the heart, and perceived by faith," and turn to God offering "up all the thoughts of our hearts, all the words of our tongues, and all the works of our hands, all our body, soul, and spirit, to be an holy sacrifice, acceptable unto God in Christ Jesus."

All: We pray for the wisdom and courage to change the ways we live and work, relate to one another and the earth, and allow our nations to be governed. Through God's grace, we renew our minds, reorient our wills, and recommit ourselves to faithful discipleship as instruments of God's renewing Spirit. We rededicate ourselves faithfully to follow the One who came into the world to reconcile us to God and to one another.

> ### Going Further
>
> - The Web site www.hopeandaction.org has other articles and stories that relate to the Pastoral Letter.
>
> - Go to www.surveymonkey.com/s/ hopeandaction and complete the survey. This survey will help the Council of Bishops to understand how the Pastoral Letter has been received and what actions individuals and congregations are taking.

Guide for Teachers of Children

For Teachers

God's Renewed Creation is a rallying voice and a demonstration of rededicated leadership by the bishops to engage, inspire, and rouse United Methodists and people of goodwill to a deeper spiritual consciousness as stewards and caretakers of Creation.

From the very beginning, God asked people to care for one another and for God's creation. The foundation of stewardship can be traced back to Creation. When people are good stewards of resources, they ensure that there will be enough for everyone.

We can help our children experience what it means to be good stewards of God's beautiful work. The following activities will help get your children thinking about the joys of caring for the world God made.

Introduction

Say: Life is a gift. It is a part of God's plan of creation. Life started from God and depends on God. God is the source and sustainer of everything.

Teach the following verse to the children:

"You let us rule everything your hands have made." (Psalm 8:6 CEV)

Repeat the verse together several times until the children are comfortable saying it.

Activity 1: Earth Tag (uses CEV Bible)

To prepare for this game, recruit one or more leaders to hold an earth ball (inflatable ball) and tag the children. Provide CEV Bibles. Place the Bibles where the children can easily access them.

Say: You will need to know today's Bible verse for this game. Let's say the Bible verse together: "You let us rule everything your hands have made." To play the game, everyone will wander around the room. Wandering with us will be someone holding an earth ball. If you are tagged with the ball, you must say today's Bible verse, then pick up a Bible, and finally sit down in front of the stage (*or other group area*).

Play Earth Tag with the children until everyone is seated.

Say: Our Bible story is from the first book in the Bible, Genesis.

Help the children find the first chapter of Genesis in their Bibles. Be sure to have older children or adults ready to help nonreaders.

Say: What are the first three words in chapter one? ("In the beginning"). "Genesis" means *beginning*. Chapter 1 tells us about the beginning of the world. Our God created an awesome universe. God created every living thing. And that includes us. When God created humans, God gave us a big responsibility. Verse 26 tells us what that responsibility is. Look at the words as I read the verse: "Then God said, 'Let us make humankind in our image, according to our likeness; and let them have dominion over the fish of the sea, and over the birds of the air, and over the cattle, and over all the wild animals of the earth, and over every creeping thing that creeps upon the earth.' "

Ask: What does the word *dominion* mean? (To rule over.)

Say: The word *dominion* reminds me of the word *rule*, and that reminds me of our Bible verse, Psalm 8:6. Let's have a race to see how fast you can find Psalm 8:6 in your Bible. If you want to come up front and be in the race, hold up your hand.

Choose four to six children to come up front. They may bring CEV Bibles or you can give them Bibles when they are on stage.

Pair the children in teams of two. If you have older and younger children, pair an older child with a younger child. Each pair needs a Bible.

Say: When I say, "Go!" work together with your partner to find the verse. As soon as you find the verse, raise your hand. Are you ready? Find Psalm 8:6. Set. That's Psalm 8:6. Go!

Encourage all the children to cheer as the partners work together to find the verse. Have the first pair to find the verse and raise their hands, read the verse. Thank the children who came to the front and have them sit down.

Ask: So what is our big responsibility? (To rule over everything God made.) Let's think about some ways we can be good rulers over creation.

Activity 2: Pick It Up

To prepare for this game, place a recycle box near the front of the group area. Space out clean recyclable trash (newspaper, plastic bottles, food boxes, and so forth) on the floor. You will need at least one piece of trash per child. Choose an adult to be the leader.

Say: Every day, the average American produces a little more than four pounds of trash. That's enough to fill over 63,000 trash trucks. If everyone in the world produced as much trash as we do, then we would need two more planets just to hold all the trash.

Ask: Where does all this trash go? (Into landfills, dumps, the ocean.)

Say: Let's play "Pick It Up." Choose a partner.

Have the children choose partners. If you have an uneven number of children in your group, partner with one of the children yourself. Point out the trash that is scattered in the group area.

Say: When (*name of leader*) **shouts, "Pick It Up!" move with your partner to one piece of trash on the floor. Listen to** (*name of leader*). **He or she will call out a body part. Then work with your partner to pick up the trash and take it to the recycling box—but you can only use that body part.**

When the leader shouts "Pick It Up!" encourage the partners to stand by a piece of trash.

When the leader calls out a body part (elbow to elbow, foot to foot, knee to knee, knee to elbow, hand to foot, and so forth) encourage the partners to pick up the trash and move it to the recycle box.

Continue the game until all the trash is placed in the recycle box.

Ask: Why is it important that we help take care of the earth? (God gave us dominion over it. If we don't do it, no one else will.)

Activity 3: Sing Together

Sing these words to the tune of "If You're Happy and You Know It":

If You're Green and You Know It

If you're green and you know it, plant a tree.
If you're green and you know it, plant a tree.
If you're green and you know it,
then your life will surely show it.
If you're green and you know it, plant a tree.

If you're green and you know it . . .
turn off lights.
save a whale.
sort the trash.
ride a bike.
love the earth.

Close by praying together.

Pray: Dear Lord, only you can instill in us the right and proper desire to be stewards of the things you have entrusted us with. Because of Jesus' sacrifice for us, we can have an awesome love for people and living things. Help us rule over the work of your hands with faithfulness and integrity. We pray these things in Jesus' name. Amen.

Recommended Resources (to help involve your children in deeper exploration of what it means to be stewards of God's creation):

Green Church: Caretakers of God's Creation by Daphna Flegal and Suzann Wade (Abingdon Press, 2010).

The Sudan Project: Rebuilding With the People of Darfur by Melissa Leembruggen (Abingdon Press, 2007).